D0759549

Zodiacal Symbology

AND ITS

PLANETARY POWER

IN WHICH THE PLANETARY INFLUENCE FOR
EACH DEGREE OF THE ZODIAC
ACCOMPANIES THE SYMBOL
FOR THE FIRST TIME

BY

ISIDORE KOZMINSKY

D.Sc., F.R.H.S., F.R.N.S., B.A.S., etc.

Author of

"Numbers, their Meaning
and Magic," etc.

Published by

American Federation of Astrologers
6 Library Court S.E.
Washington, D. C. 20003

PREFACE

AFTER some years of careful study in the endeavour to fix the special planetary influence attached to each degree of the Zodiac, I am at length enabled to present the result of my researches in this direction for the consideration of the many sincere students who find in astrology a safe and sure foundation upon which to build the temple of world enlightenment, which the approaching true civilization will demand. From a close examination of thousands of nativities during the past, I have reason to believe that the planets which will be found associated with the zodiacal degrees in this book are correct and important in every particular. I believe this is the first attempt in this direction, and I am sure that it will be found helpful in dealing with the many problems with which the student has to grapple. Especially will it be useful in determining, together with the associated symbol, the special degree of the Zodiac which rises at the birth, when time is given with no measure of certainty, and as an aid to prenatal and other astrological considerations.

5

PREFACE

I may here remark that I always consider the degree rising as belonging to the degree following, when the merest fraction over indicates to me its claim. For example, 1°1′♈ is ♈2°, etc. I am noting this because some practitioners do not regard the change until 30′ and over past the exact degree. Apart from the old Quabbalistical symbols associated with certain interpretations, some of which are dealt with in my book on " Numbers, their Meaning and Magic," and kindred works ; the magical symbols in Comte de Glenstrae's " Book of Sacred Magic " ; " Symbols of Hermetic Philosophy," by Eliphas Levi ; " Rosicrucian Symbols," by Antonio Ginther (eighteenth century) ; " Symbols of the Mansions of the Moon," by Francis Barrett ; " Symbols on Antique and Gnostic Gems," by Rev. C. W. King —I know only of the excellent translation of " La Volasfera," by Sepharial, the set by Johannes Angelus (sixteenth century) published by Raphael, those by the venerable Charubel, and the Symbols of the Decanates in the " Brihat Jataka." The " Romance of Symbolism," by Sidney Heath, " Migration of Symbols," by Comte d'Alviella of Belgium, and works of a like nature, are only concerned with Church Symbology and have no special connexion with the symbols of the Zodiac. The Bible, in common with other great magical

6

books, is full of symbol and parable. The ancient method of imparting magical, philosophical, and ethical knowledge employed by the Great Masters was by emblem, parable, and symbol; and the religious orders from the earliest times have not been slow to grasp the intensity of its import, and to employ it to the utmost. Having the evidence of the mighty past before me, and a full realization of the mystic majesty of symbolic lore, I feel that I am not wrong in saying that no form of religious worship ever endured without it, and no form of religious worship ever will. The mere word passages are as nothing compared with the magical influence of a symbol before the eyes of the devotional. Hence we have Winged Bulls, Sphinxes, Pyramids, Dragons, Globes, Crosses, planetary symbols based on the evolution of the human soul right down to those employed by William Lilly in his warning of the Plague and Fire of London, and by other famous scholars of past days. Some ages have passed since the days of the week were named, and the symbols attached to them appear in some old works, though they are seldom quoted now. Thus for Sunday—the day of the Sun—Apollo's day, we have the symbol of the Solar rays issuing from the head of the Sun-god. For Monday—the day of the Moon— we have the symbol of a Bear. This name, in

7

ancient times, was applied to a young virgin in referring to her protective goddess Luna or Diana. For Tuesday—the day of Tew or Ty (Mars)— we have the symbol of an Arrow-head. For Wednesday—the day of Woden or Wuotan (Mercury)—we have the symbol of the Triskele. For Thursday—the day of Thor (Jupiter)—we have the symbol of a Hammer or a Fylfot Cross. The rowan-tree is known as Thor's aid because, so the story goes, it bent towards him, enabling him to hold it when, on his way to the land of the Frost Giants, he had to cross a river in flood. For Friday—the day of Freya (Venus)—we have the Cross Pattée; and for Saturday—the day of Saturnus—we have the Sickle. In the Eleusinian mysteries, the symbol of an ear of corn reaped in silence was presented to the aspirant as a most sacred emblem of mystery. It is unnecessary now to delve deeper into the forests of symbology, else amidst its many intricacies we may miss our way, for so very deep is it, and so alluring to the traveller its fantastic paths. Later we may explore, but not now. It is better to raise our eyes to the stars in the heavens and draw from them some of that immensity of knowledge stored within them, and we may be well assured that if in this incarnation we gather a few grains of sand from the myriads of grains on that long, wide, and

8

PREFACE

beautiful beach, we have done well and have prepared the way for our entrance into a realm before which all the fantastic legends of the Arabian Nights fade into the comparative insignificance of ill-remembered dreams.

ISIDORE KOZMINSKY

31 Dalgety Street, St. Kilda,
    Melbourne, Victoria, Australia

Note

For purposes of convenience the masculine gender is used in the interpretation of the symbols.

Zodiacal Symbology and its Planetary Power

ARIES

♈

♈ 1°. UNDER THE INFLUENCE OF THE PLANET URANUS.

A ball of fire bursting across a rainbow.

Denotes one of strength, force, and daring. By nature he is aggressive and martial, desiring to conquer at all costs. He is restless and impelling, taking many risks and enduring many hardships. The degree is a dangerous one, threatening mind and body. The symbol is a symbol of Action.

♈ 2°. UNDER THE INFLUENCE OF THE PLANET URANUS.

A man with a sword in his hand falling through a skylight of coloured glass.

Denotes one of a rash and impetuous nature. He is strong and brave, but is wanting in restraint,

11

and is apt to involve himself in unpopular or regrettable actions. Such a one will, all through life, have to exercise a strong hand over himself and his actions. It is a symbol of Rashness.

♈ 3°. UNDER THE INFLUENCE OF THE PLANET MARS.

A prince saving a child from a burning castle.
Denotes one of brave and noble qualities whose sense of duty holds danger in contempt when the call is for the help of the weak. As a leader such a one can be relied on in any emergency which may arise. He aims high materially and spiritually. It is a symbol of Nobility.

♈ 4°. UNDER THE INFLUENCE OF THE PLANET MARS.

A mailed hand holding a dagger with a bent point.
Denotes one protected against external hurt, yet who, with a powerful desire for martial action in all affairs of life, may be tempted to use protective armour for offensive purposes, forgetting that the point of the dagger of aggression is blunted. Such a one needs to restrain impulse and to bestow thought and study on any contemplated action, then let him be sure that his dagger be true before he strikes. It is a symbol of Misconception.

12

♈ 5°. UNDER THE INFLUENCE OF THE PLANET
VENUS.

*A feudal knight in full armour standing on
the walls of his castle defying a multitude of
armed people—a mysterious figure at the back
of the crowd strikes a note on a curious six-
stringed harp, the massive walls crumble and
fall, and the defier is at the mercy of the defied.*

Denotes one who is apt to place infinite reliance
on materialistic things and to exult in the strength
which their possession gives him over the masses
of men.   In the midst of his power a spiritual
force, acting on invisible agencies and sending
forth a note softer than the trumpet sounds of
Jericho, may rudely disturb him.   Then, if his
soul truly awakes, the native becomes a valiant
knight in the cause of enlightenment, but if the
soul slumbers back again into the sludge of
materialism, then will the native again place all
his hopes on things that seem, and the defier will
be truly at the mercy of the defied.   It is a symbol
of False Security.

♈ 6°. UNDER THE INFLUENCE OF THE PLANET
VENUS.

*A metalsmith in his workshop fixing a silver
caduceus of Mercury in a base of copper.*

13

Around are scattered various metals and instruments.

Denotes one of inward understanding. The smith by his craft glorifies the power of love and intelligence which he cements together. The base of copper indicates that no form of learning matters unless it is engendered by love and held by its soft and holy influence. One with this degree rising has a noble destiny. He is the metalsmith, and this is the mark of his mission. It is a symbol of Mental Perception.

♈ 7°. UNDER THE INFLUENCE OF THE PLANET VENUS.

A man saving himself from falling into a deep cavern by clutching a wild rose-tree. The thorns cut into his flesh, but the plant supports him.

Denotes one lacking self-confidence, relying too much on the weaker things which wound him whilst they hold him. To this native, luxury is hurtful, for the senses are active and the feelings quickly respond to environment. To rise superior to external conditions and the tyranny of sense is the task of the native of this degree. The symbol is a symbol of Weakness.

ARIES

♈ 8°. UNDER THE INFLUENCE OF THE PLANET MERCURY.

A silver axe shattering a shield of iron.

Denotes one possessing understanding and a penetrative intellect who will be compelled many times in life to exert his abilities for the removal of obstacles and formidable enemies. He is gifted with much moral bravery and a high sense of duty. Here we have a hero whose weapon of defence and offence is the mind. It is a symbol of Penetration.

♈ 9°. UNDER THE INFLUENCE OF THE PLANET MERCURY.

A Roman general gaudily apparelled receiving a wreath of flowers from an empress.

Denotes one of proud bearing who delights in fine clothes and display. He will always attract admirers, and gain honour and advancement. In some way he will bear rule. If fate leads him into the theatrical profession, he will lead. If into business, he will be strong, courted, and successful in finance. If into the army or navy he will be a powerful officer. It is a symbol of Gaining.

♈ 10°. UNDER THE INFLUENCE OF THE MOON.
A ship illumined with the rosy rays of morning sailing towards the rising sun.

Denotes spiritual and material advancement. The native will in some way be a pioneer whose labours will be hailed and recognized. He will be favoured by the people, and will easily attract influence. To obtain the best promises of this degree he may have to move about as indicated in his horoscope. It is a symbol of Influence.

♈ 11°. UNDER THE INFLUENCE OF THE MOON.
A little child tying a ribbon round a lamb's neck, the flock playfully frolicking around.

Denotes one of simple manners and lovable personality who has the power to change sadness into joy and wipe away tears from the faces of the afflicted. One to whom trust is given and who will not abuse it. It is a symbol of Ideality.

♈ 12°. UNDER THE INFLUENCE OF THE MOON.
A Druid cutting the acorn from the sacred oak with a sickle of silver.

Denotes change and romance. The native will suffer fluctuations in thoughts, feelings, and conditions. As the body ages, the higher side of the native asserts itself and the allurements of

16

youth fail to hold power over him. Much wandering and many strange adventures make up his experiences in the worlds spiritual and material. It is a symbol of Roaming.

♈ 13°. Under the influence of the sun.

A bright steel cross-sword with a handle of gleaming copper, above it a heart of gold from which stream shafts of golden light.

Denotes bravery, love, and sincerity. Honour will come to this native, his thoughts and ambitions lead him upwards. By Love's guidance he passes over obstacles and pursues an honorable course. His nature is somewhat proud, but he is generous and noble-minded. Influence and favour come to him. It is a symbol of Light.

♈ 14°. Under the influence of the sun.

A man standing on a mountain gazing sadly on the valley below, where some men are fighting for a bag of gold whilst a monkey is eating their food. On his right is the spirit of Truth : on his left the spirit of Error ; seated at his feet is the spirit of Love ; behind him, holding on to his garment, is the spirit of Hate.

Denotes one who reaches a position of responsibility, power, and influence, and seeks to find in

17

man the spark which being agitated blazes forth in glory, guiding by its perfect light. Here we have the teacher who strives to lead men from the valley of darkness into the light of understanding, but who himself is threatened by Error and Hate, which if he permits to influence him will drag him from his throne. But if he join his own great soul to Truth and Love, what wonders may he not perform! It is a symbol of Intercession.

♈ 15°. UNDER THE INFLUENCE OF THE PLANET MERCURY.

A Crusading knight with red cross on white corselet sinking in the quicksands, an Arab mocking at him from the safe ground he has left.

Denotes an adventurer or one who follows risk and courts trouble, for he carries the cross of suffering on a field of light. He may be gifted with some noble sentiments, feelings, and impressions, but his very rashness and impetuosity force him to miscalculate, threatening to make him the sport of his enemies. It is a symbol of Deviation.

18

ARIES

♈ 16°. UNDER THE INFLUENCE OF THE PLANET MERCURY.

Wild flowers growing amidst the corn in a sunlit field.

Denotes a person of charm, a lover of freedom—mental and physical—of nature, and of simple loveliness whose works in life will be blessed with success, and whose individuality will make itself felt amongst men. It is a symbol of Abundance.

♈ 17°. UNDER THE INFLUENCE OF THE PLANET MERCURY.

A beautiful woman, richly dressed, reclining on a couch, with fruits and golden vessels around her. At her hand, on an ornate table of white marble, lies an opened book.

Denotes a lotus-eater, a lover of pleasure, who delights in ease and the sweets of life. The fortunes are favoured, but the native makes no personal effort to increase them. The mind is romantic and art-loving, and the form graceful. It is a symbol of Luxury.

♈ 18°. UNDER THE INFLUENCE OF THE PLANET VENUS.

The goddess Venus holding out her hands to a

19

wounded soldier, who is painfully trying to reach her.

Denotes sympathy. Many times will the native stumble and fall by the way, but ever will there be a bright light before him to dispel the darkness of the night and to dissipate his fears. The mind is aspiring, but to reach its ideal, pain and struggle are involved. The native must not falter, for very nigh unto him is his hope—a little sacrifice and endeavour will unite him to it. It is a symbol of Upraising.

♈ 19°. UNDER THE INFLUENCE OF THE PLANET VENUS.

A harp resting against an altar, from which a volume of smoke arises.

Denotes one whose soul is full of poetry, harmony, and true religion, whose endeavours may be thwarted, but not suppressed. One to whom peace and goodwill are more precious than mere words, and whose prayers are unselfish, thought-ful, and sincere. It is a symbol of Consecration.

♈ 20°. UNDER THE INFLUENCE OF THE PLANET MARS.

A blacksmith hammering a piece of red-hot iron on an anvil.

Denotes a determined worker, vigorous in the

fight against opposition—a transmuter of himself and those who contend against him. Gifted with so strong a spirit, this native can never be mean. Baseness does not find a place in his nature. He loathes idleness, for energy, pain, and experience have taught him the power of industry. It is a symbol of Resolution.

♈ 21°. UNDER THE INFLUENCE OF THE PLANET MARS.

A man struggling with a fierce serpent whilst others armed with large knives are hurrying to aid him.

Denotes one who will be assailed by secret and open enemies, who will be liable to troubles and false accusations. In his dealings he should always exercise great care, and should not rely on word-of-mouth agreements. He will not be without devoted friends, who will not neglect him in the hour of his greatest need. His intense feelings will cause him trouble, danger, illness, and regret, and he will have to strive with the dark serpent. Let him unite himself with noble and good-living people, and put away from himself votaries of evil. It is a symbol of Contention.

ZODIACAL SYMBOLOGY

♈ 22°. UNDER THE INFLUENCE OF THE PLANET MARS.

A pilgrim crossing himself in front of an ancient temple, an overdressed official and a soldier mocking at him.

Denotes a devout person who will be subjected to many trials and taunts in life, but who will, by the strength of his faith, overcome them all. He comes from the masses rather than from the classes, and his sympathy will ever be with the struggling people of the nations. From officialdom and materialism he receives scant courtesy. It is a symbol of Faith.

♈ 23°. UNDER THE INFLUENCE OF THE PLANET JUPITER.

A king absorbed in the flatteries of a courtier whose mistress is stealing important documents from a drawer.

Denotes one who is too ready to delude himself and to live in an insincere atmosphere of adulation and deception. Without accomplishing anything of particular merit, he accepts praises from flattering parasites. Thus is he lulled into a sense of false security, and loses those things which are truly of worth. It is a symbol of Entrapping.

ARIES

♈ 24°. Under the influence of the planet
Jupiter.

*A youth grasping a beautiful woman, who
turns into a skeleton in his arms.*

Denotes one who may lose his way following his
desires. He is highly passionate, and allows
himself to be shaken by his senses as the wind
shakes the autumn leaves. He is then apt to
grow selfish, and to disregard the feelings and
rights of others, with consequences bringing to
him death, defeat, and disaster. It is a symbol
of Illusion.

♈ 25°. Under the influence of the planet
Saturn.

*An old man with a scythe cutting down a
field of nettles.*

Denotes one who cuts his way through pricks,
scratches, and wounds. The " coldly useful "
may rise up against him to again be cut down to
his advantage. The native is not tied to mere
sentiment, and will be keen and enthusiastic in
research, leading to discovery. It is a symbol of
Revealing.

ZODIACAL SYMBOLOGY

♈ 26°. UNDER THE INFLUENCE OF THE PLANET
SATURN.

> *The governor of a city surrendering the keys
> to a dark frowning conqueror.*

Denotes one who struggles bravely against great
odds who is beset by enemies who harass and
worry him. After a great fight he may have to
hand over what he holds to one stronger than he
is and be content with what consideration is
given to him afterwards. It is a symbol of
Dependence.

♈ 27°. UNDER THE INFLUENCE OF THE PLANET
SATURN.

> *A huge hour-glass, the sands in which are
> running low.*

Denotes one who is apt to delay the following up
of matters of importance and to procrastinate
until the hour grows too late to serve his purposes.
His tendency is to move too slowly when the
nature of an event demands hasty action. It is
a symbol of Delaying.

♈ 28°. UNDER THE INFLUENCE OF THE PLANET
URANUS.

> *A lapidary holding in his hand a magnificent
> amethyst, at which he gazes admiringly.*

Denotes one gifted with mental and moral
24

strength, power, and forcefulness, who brings hope to many a sad or fearful heart. He is magnetic and iconoclastic, and by his faith and will he gains many adherents. It is a symbol of Fascination.

♈ 29°.   UNDER THE INFLUENCE OF THE PLANET URANUS.

An artist laying a mosaic pavement in a large public building. He works slowly and with great patience.

Denotes one of refined and patient nature who is content to work hard and slowly in the endeavour to accomplish worthy and enduring objects. He may be skilled in the arts that uplift, or an admirer of them. Still his destiny is bright, especially after his forty-fifth year, when his merit will receive recognition and favour. It is a symbol of Development.

♈ 30°.   UNDER THE INFLUENCE OF THE PLANET NEPTUNE.

A man endeavouring to subdue a raging forest fire with a pail of water.

Denotes one who will endure sorrow and who underestimates the strength of his adversaries. He is apt to enter into great schemes with very

25

little backing, and to provoke argument without being prepared to meet it. Hence he is continually at the mercy of forces into whose grip he enters without regard to consequences. He is apt to fight a hard fight with insignificant weapons, and thus to court defeat. It is a symbol of Unreadiness.

TAURUS

♉

UNDER THE INFLUENCE OF THE PLANET
NEPTUNE.

*A grey vapour surrounding a bush of red roses
upon which is a brilliantly coloured butterfly.*

Denotes one whose life is threatened in early
infancy. The ideals are high, and he delights in
all that is beautiful and sweet. The native is
somewhat erratic and inconstant, loving " fresh
fields and pastures new." He inclines to the
poetic and artistic, and may excel in such paths.
It is a symbol of Cultivation.

♉ 2°. UNDER THE INFLUENCE OF THE PLANET
NEPTUNE.

*A heart crowned on the summit of a barren rock
jutting out of the ocean—a bevy of white sea-
birds speeding towards it from the east in
crescent form.*

Denotes one capable of immense sacrifices who
surrenders self, expecting no reward. The life

27

will be often lonely, but ever threatened by storms. In the end wisdom and worth will triumph and the second half of life brings good promise. It is a symbol of Devotion.

♉ 3°. UNDER THE INFLUENCE OF THE PLANET VENUS.

A man tossing handfuls of seed to the earth, which, as soon as they touch, fructify and incline towards him.

Denotes one favoured by fortune. He will possess good judgment, and will do the right thing at the right time. His early life will be filled with struggle and with promise, expanding to favour as he advances in years. With a good insight into human nature the native can well choose others to assist in his work, and whilst holding work to be the true necessity of life, he knows the value of relaxation and pleasure to others as to himself. It is a symbol of Fortune.

♉ 4°. UNDER THE INFLUENCE OF THE PLANET VENUS.

The arena of a circus during a night perform-ance, the ringmaster in the centre urging forward the movements of a large white horse galloping round the ring, a lady gymnast standing on the animal's back holding a hoop of fire.

Denotes one whose destiny it is to come before the public in some professional capacity. The native will be impulsive, bold, and brave, and will be gifted with controlling and magnetic force. He will travel and move about a great deal, and will be exposed to danger with little or no hurt. It is a symbol of Intrepidity.

♉ 5°. UNDER THE INFLUENCE OF THE PLANET MERCURY.

Two young men carrying huge bunches of large grapes on a pole between them, giving freely of the fruit to troops of children.

Denotes one who will gain greatly through his own efforts and perseverance, and who will be blessed. He will bring happiness to, and relieve the burden of, many, accounting it pleasure. Thus will he draw unto himself the good thoughts and prayers of others. It is a symbol of Benefaction.

♉ 6°. UNDER THE INFLUENCE OF THE PLANET MERCURY.

A judge in his robes of office handing a book to a student, who is stretching out his hands to receive it.

Denotes one who will rise to a position of importance, and whose mission and ambition it will be in life to give instruction and to secure the advancement of worthy people of wit, talent, and inspiration. These acts will reflect his own glory as the Moon reflects the brightness of the Sun. It is a symbol of Illumination.

♉ 7°. UNDER THE INFLUENCE OF THE PLANET MERCURY.

> *A beautiful white swan swimming on a smooth lake edged by lilies and grasses and pretty little wild flowers.*

Denotes a tranquil and romantic life. The native is gifted poetically, and can express his feelings in the book of Nature with charming simplicity. He will not have much to trouble him in the world of men, and should keep away from crowds and mixed atmospheres, as he is singularly sensitive to external conditions. It is a symbol of Tranquillity.

♉ 8°. UNDER THE INFLUENCE OF THE MOON.

> *A leafless tree, on a plain, bending before a violent gale of wind, which whistles wildly through the branches.*

Denotes one who meets with opposition, obstacles, and trouble who will be compelled to battle
30

against adversity. Such a one should never take risks in anything, no matter how promising, but be content to work on in the very teeth of the enemy, remembering always that the strong are chosen to fight the battles of the weak. It is a symbol of Impediment.

♉ 9°. UNDER THE INFLUENCE OF THE MOON.

A farmer driving a cart filled with fruit, at which birds are pecking.

Denotes one who acquires much by work and application, but who lacks the faculty of watchfulness in protecting his gains from the greed of others. He has an easygoing tendency, but gains come from labour, craft, and the management of his own affairs. He may be the victim of deceit or treachery, and should never put himself in the hands of others when his own well-being is concerned. He should avoid things and circumstances he does not understand. It is a symbol of Misleading.

♉ 10°. UNDER THE INFLUENCE OF THE SUN.

A daintily dressed woman sitting by a placid lake, gazing intently at a man's face reflected in the water.

Denotes a person of refined tastes and feelings,

gifted with clairvoyant power and artistic skill. A union with one of psychic power—a soul-mate —brings harmony or complications (as indicated in the nativity) into a life which commands power and influence. It is a symbol of Descrying.

♉ 11°.   UNDER THE INFLUENCE OF THE SUN.

A monk on a rocky road giving drink and food to a poor traveller who has fallen by the way. A rayed anchor above his head.

Denotes one of religious and charitable nature whose high understanding of the brotherhood of man and the absolute unity of human aims, when not diverted by the evil powers, makes him ever ready to divide his substance with those who, less fortunate in worldly matters, give a higher payment—human blessings and gratitude. His trust in humanity is never shaken. He is ever to others a harbinger of hope. It is a symbol of Deliverance.

♉ 12°.   UNDER THE INFLUENCE OF THE SUN.

Two diggers working on a mountain-slope unearth a large mass of glittering gold.

Denotes one of a searching nature who knows the true value of sincere work. He will never spare himself until his purpose is achieved. With him

32

persistence wins by virtue of his fate. It is a symbol of Endurance.

♉ 13°. UNDER THE INFLUENCE OF THE PLANET MERCURY.

A judge in a court of law frowning at a man holding up a document.

Denotes one who is energetic and active, but who is threatened with disfavour, prejudice, and adverse judgment. He has trials in life, and suffers much, and he is likely to oppose or be opposed by authority. If Mercury is weak or afflicted in the horoscope, the native suffers in business and from law; but if this planet is strong he is a mental pioneer fighting for liberty. It is a symbol of Gripping.

♉ 14°. UNDER THE INFLUENCE OF THE PLANET MERCURY.

A virgin clothed in white, with a bright star above her head, joining the hands of two men about to quarrel.

Denotes one whose love of harmony adds to the beauty of a spiritual nature. To him there is no virtue higher than peace, and nothing so unworthy of man's high mission as inharmony and hate. Gifted with a sweet and lovable personality and

33

fine magnetic force, his power is felt and respected. It is a symbol of Harmonious Love.

♉ 15°.   UNDER THE INFLUENCE OF THE PLANET VENUS.

> *A student with lamp in hand, standing at the entrance of a cavern from which issue clouds of soft, light, rosy vapour.*

Denotes a person whose tastes and desires are directed to the understanding of the secrets which rest beneath the veil. He has brought to earth from other sources the knowledge which enables him to find the entrance to the cavern of hidden jewels, but it is doubtful if he can enter, for the gateway is guarded by sublime and intense colours caused by more excessive vibrations than can be endured by the human body. The light vapour approaching the " Ultra " stage is more powerful and effective than dragons of fire. It is a symbol of Initiation.

♉ 16°.   UNDER THE INFLUENCE OF THE PLANET VENUS.

> *A white dove, adorned with a rose-coloured ribbon to which is attached a little bell, standing on the right shoulder of a man drinking wine.*

Denotes one of a merry and convivial spirit who

34

will be favoured by women and Venus. There is a tendency to too much indulgence, but ever a restraining power which holds the native to a right and rosy course. It is a symbol of Good Living.

♉ 17°. UNDER THE INFLUENCE OF THE PLANET MARS.

A sea-gull flying over the waters of the ocean.

Denotes one free as air, brave, spiritual, restless, and unfitted for the regular routine of daily life. Care in infancy is essential. He is of a wandering disposition and frequent changes are for him. It is a symbol of Wandering.

♉ 18°. UNDER THE INFLUENCE OF THE PLANET MARS.

A gaudily dressed herald blowing a trumpet, at the sound of which two knights, one on a white charger, the other on a black, rush towards each other with set spears.

Denotes one of a strongly martial disposition who delights in struggle and contention. He has a love of show and glitter, and desires to make himself heard. Within him is a continual war between good and evil, and victory depends on himself alone. It is a symbol of Combativeness.

ZODIACAL SYMBOLOGY

♉ 19°. UNDER THE INFLUENCE OF THE PLANET
MARS.

*An archer, dressed in red, firing arrows at the
Moon.*

Denotes one who is unable to estimate his abilities
and who attempts things foolhardy and useless.
There is a tendency to irritability and aggressive-
ness and lack of self-restraint. Thus he will
court unpopularity and will suffer from his own
actions. It is a symbol of Futility.

♉ 20°. UNDER THE INFLUENCE OF THE PLANET
JUPITER.

A flight of white eagles.

Denotes one whose thoughts are high and whose
ambitions are serenely regulated. He rises in
life, gaining command and respect. He is far-
seeing, and his virtues enable him to accomplish
good work in this world. It is a symbol of
Celebrity.

♉ 21°. UNDER THE INFLUENCE OF THE PLANET
JUPITER.

*A race-horse with the number 3 on his saddle-
cloth entering a course.*

Denotes one of sporting tendencies who delights
in trials of skill and who is generally fortunate.
36

TAURUS

To his nature there is a generous, sympathetic, and interesting side, which gains him many friends and much popularity. It is a symbol of Sportiveness.

♉ 22°. UNDER THE INFLUENCE OF THE PLANET JUPITER.

Hand holding a torch amidst the darkness.

Denotes a lightbearer whose mission is to guide others and to uplift them. No matter how dark the way, his presence inspires brightness. There is no weakness in this native, who knows just what he is on this world to do and who does it. It is a symbol of Directorship.

♉ 23°. UNDER THE INFLUENCE OF THE PLANET SATURN.

St. Michael slaying the Dragon in a shower of black rain.

Denotes one with strength of purpose and ability to sustain trials. The Dragon is lust, corruption, and the cold moistures of the earth. St. Michael is the life, solar energy, conqueror of decay; the black rain the evil which corruption draws. So when the native realizes his soul force he becomes a veritable victor over the monster into whose

37

jaws so many unwarned and unguarded fall.
It is a symbol of Victory.

♉ 24°. UNDER THE INFLUENCE OF THE PLANET
SATURN.

*A prisoner having escaped from his prison is
endeavouring to break his fetters with the aid
of some large flinty stones.*

Denotes one whose life is harassed by other
people, and who will be held to a position to his
disadvantage from which he will free himself
and go where better conditions prevail, and where
he will have better opportunities for employing
his skill for his own good. Consult the horoscope.
It is a symbol of Restraining.

♉ 25°. UNDER THE INFLUENCE OF THE PLANET
URANUS.

*A dense column of smoke from which issue
flashes of lightning.*

Denotes one of natural talent who will be beset
with difficulties in gaining recognition, but whose
mental strength will be the more determined
because of them. When his time comes his power
will be felt. He will force acknowledgment by
sheer ability and energy. It is a symbol of
Premeditation.

38

TAURUS

♉ 26°. UNDER THE INFLUENCE OF THE PLANET URANUS.

A giant of benevolent aspect, with his foot on a broken sword, tearing up the laws of the world by which men have been governed for centuries. Behind him are broken bags of golden coins, which are falling in a shower over a precipice.

Denotes a child of the new age whose thoughts contend against orthodoxy, systems, war, and the accepted justice of the times. He is gifted with a powerful and convincing individuality, strong in wisdom, worth, and excellence. His mind is dominant, and he is morally and mentally brave. It is a symbol of Iconoclasm.

♉ 27°. UNDER THE INFLUENCE OF THE PLANET URANUS.

An inventor having risen from his bench gazes admiringly at a remarkable engine which he has just completed.

Denotes one who will produce work of value to the race. He is gifted with inventive ability and a quick mind, and will concrete ideas whilst others are but dreaming of them. It is a symbol of Ingenuity.

39

ZODIACAL SYMBOLOGY

♉ 28°. UNDER THE INFLUENCE OF THE PLANET NEPTUNE.

A woman looking into a crystal ball in which confused images are reflected.

Denotes a mediumistic person who, for lack of energetic study and cultivation, has difficulty in understanding the true value and meaning of the messages which he receives. To such a one long study and care will bring repayment. But self-sacrifice is demanded. It is a symbol of Disorder.

♉ 29°. UNDER THE INFLUENCE OF THE PLANET NEPTUNE.

A man at a cross-road. Above him are two spirits, one black and the other white. Each strives to impress him, but his mind is too perplexed to understand either.

Denotes one who is continually beset with difficulties and who finds it hard at all times to decide his course of action. He is ever between forces of opposite natures, and is quite as likely to do the right thing as the wrong one. These conditions must be subdued by the steady cultivation of the will. It is a symbol of Embarrassment.

TAURUS

♉ 30°. UNDER THE INFLUENCE OF THE PLANET MARS.

A huge ironstone rolling down a mountain-side strikes a clump of hard flint, causing a bright fiery flash.

Denotes a venturesome and determined spirit who will dare and do much to attain his ambitions. The earlier life will be filled with struggles and beset with difficulties which, as he advances in years, will enable him to gain the experience necessary to make his name known and his ideas respected. It is a symbol of Forcefulness.

GEMINI

♊

♊ 1°. UNDER THE INFLUENCE OF THE PLANET
MARS.

*Two Ionic columns adorned with globes—a
burst of flame issuing out of clouds behind.*

Denotes a double-natured, cultured, and gifted
person who gains reputation through his acts.
He has great mental energy and will, combined
with an impetuosity which directs to good or evil
results. His overhastiness may lead him to
mistakes which incur displeasure and court
danger. It is a symbol of Animation.

♊ 2°. UNDER THE INFLUENCE OF THE PLANET
MARS.

*A military officer seated on a heap of arms
studying a map which he holds in his hands.*

Denotes one of much discrimination and capacity
for study, with ability to lead and direct others.
His movements are guided by knowledge and
moulded by study. Danger seems to have a

42

fascination for him; for, conscious of his own ability to surmount difficulties, he has little fear even in the midst of strife. It is a symbol of Unravelling.

♊ 3°. UNDER THE INFLUENCE OF THE PLANET MERCURY.

A composer standing before a large organ, with a scroll of music in his hand.

Denotes one who will serve and elevate the public and who will be a master in his own particular work. Gifted with intense idealism and the true understanding of values in his special sphere, he will gain recognition and honours in life. It is a symbol of Elegance.

♊ 4°. UNDER THE INFLUENCE OF THE PLANET MERCURY.

A human face, the expression calm and serene, a silvery triangle pointing upwards below, a dark square above.

Denotes one of spirituality and kindness who meets with trials and who is pressed under the rough heel of materialism and the greed of the world. Even so, the serene aura will flow from him as water down a mountain slope, cultivating those who come near. The conscience is strong,

43

and he loathes evil and unworthy actions. This is a peculiar degree, and certain horoscopes will force an entirely opposite interpretation. It is a symbol of Transcendentalism.

♊ 5°. UNDER THE INFLEUNCE OF THE MOON.

Little children playing near an old wrecked ship on the seashore.

Denotes one of gentle and romantic nature who will have many difficulties and troubles, reverses, and hopes destroyed, but who strives in the face of it all, unable to sink into baseness to gain worldly comforts. Later in life the native will have a period of pleasantness, and he passes from earth away from the busy cities of the world. It is a symbol of Concord.

♊ 6°. UNDER THE INFLUENCE OF THE MOON.

An analytical chemist holding up to the light a test-tube in which is a dull green liquid.

Denotes one of scientific and cautious mind, fond of experiment and research. Whether recognized by authority or not, this native never leaves his work unfinished, nor will he depart from this planet without adding rays for the progressive enlightenment of its peoples. It is a symbol of Research.

44

♊ 7°. UNDER THE INFLUENCE OF THE MOON.

A white ship with sails set on a peaceful ocean, over which the full moon is throwing a silvery light.

Denotes one of a serenely peaceful temperament, gifted with a fine imagination and creative endowment. His influence is soothing, no matter where he may be, and many are attracted to him. Generally his undertakings are successful, and he may travel much. It is a symbol of Calmness.

♊ 8°. UNDER THE INFLUENCE OF THE SUN.

A winged horse in mid-air with the Sun above its head.

Denotes an ambitious person of proud, aspiring nature, who seeks to rise, and who desires honour and reputation. The native has a good grip of human nature, its virtues, and its weaknesses, and he may find a position in some branch of the public service or in the service of his country. It is a symbol of Elevation.

♊ 9°. UNDER THE INFLUENCE OF THE SUN.

A hand holding a document on which is a crown and royal seal.

Denotes a judge, magistrate, or one who attains

45

dignity and rank, and who will be entrusted with work of delicacy and responsibility. He will enjoy much favour and many advantages during a life of more than average span. It is a symbol of Jurisdiction.

♊ 10°. UNDER THE INFLUENCE OF THE PLANET MERCURY.

A hospital nurse whose face expresses sympathy and sacrifice, tending a sick man.

Denotes one of sweetness, charity, and worth, who would sacrifice self and self's desires to aid the suffering and unfortunate. Happy and cheerful in the midst of the deepest darkness, this one will be to our race a blessing and an honour. It is a symbol of Cherishing.

♊ 11°. UNDER THE INFLUENCE OF THE PLANET MERCURY.

Interior of a stock exchange, a number of men shouting, jostling each other, and holding up papers.

Denotes one of speculative tendency who endures pain for the chance of gain, and who has much fighting and anxiety in the pursuit. He may find that, after all, the " game " is not worth while, and that the energy expended could be more profitably employed in more useful work. It is a symbol of Hazard.

♊ 12°. UNDER THE INFLUENCE OF THE PLANET MERCURY.

An accountant puzzling over a ledger, which he is struggling to balance.

Denotes one of mathematical mind who is apt to consider the various questions which arise in everyday life, and to accept nothing without strict examination and thought. He may often be considered stubborn and unyielding, but no one will more readily agree to the truth or falsity of a matter when clear evidence makes it possible for him to do so. It is a symbol of Exactness.

♊ 13°. UNDER THE INFLUENCE OF THE PLANET VENUS.

Two men playing at cards, a man standing behind one player making signs to his opponent.

Denotes one exposed to treachery and deceit who will incline to place too much reliance on those unworthy of his confidence. Care in the choice of friends should be his constant charge, nor should he indulge in ventures of a risky nature at the suggestion of any one, nor put himself in the power of any man. It is a symbol of Deceit.

♊ 14°. UNDER THE INFLUENCE OF THE PLANET VENUS.

A man in a forest handing to another an open box full of jewels which he has just stolen from an adjacent castle.

Denotes one who will be called upon to suffer from the acts of others with whom he is or has been associated. Through taking big risks he may succeed in gaining wealth, but he will be the victim of his own thoughts and the acts of his associates. It is a symbol of Entanglement.

♊ 15°. UNDER THE INFLUENCE OF THE PLANET MARS.

A wounded soldier drawing an arrow from his arm. A dog is howling near-by.

Denotes one of martial and impulsive nature who is liable to suffer from his restless temperament. His imagination is prolific, but apt to run into wrong grooves and useless pathways. To such, self-restraint and mental training is necessary, and a determination to employ his martial powers for high achievements. It is a symbol of Restlessness.

GEMINI

♊ 16°. UNDER THE INFLUENCE OF THE PLANET MARS.

A sword lying shattered before a cross of stone.

Denotes one who upholds the doctrine of sacrifice and faith above the boasted influence of force, and who will be enabled or fated to prove of himself that aggression shatters itself, whilst true faith rests unbroken and immovable. It is a symbol of Spiritual Victory.

♊ 17°. UNDER THE INFLUENCE OF THE PLANET MARS.

A blind giant in full armour hitting out wildly with a huge battle-axe at nothing.

Denotes one who overestimates his power and who rushes into quarrels from which no good can be obtained. After trouble and waste of energy he may find to his chagrin that he has gained nothing by his adventures but the reward of folly. It is a symbol of Blundering.

♊ 18°. UNDER THE INFLUENCE OF THE PLANET JUPITER.

An eagle wounded in flight swoops to a mountain ridge, where a brood of young ones rise from the drops of blood.

Denotes one of great bravery who, feeling himself
49

unconquerable, becomes a mark for the attacks of his enemies, who, thinking to smite him at the point of his weakness, raise about themselves the power which arises from his pain.   It is a symbol of Invulnerability.

♊ 19°.   Under the influence of the planet Jupiter.

> *A mountaineer, climbing in the darkness in a violent storm which has blown away his cloak and hat, saved from falling down a precipice by a flash of lightning.*

Denotes one whose vocation is one of danger and technique and who is compelled to labour under most uncomfortable conditions. He will be forced to surrender much, and will often find himself in extremely difficult positions.   Eventually he will be enabled to recover himself, and be saved from disaster by a miracle of fortunate happenings. It is a symbol of Interposition.

♊ 20°.   Under the influence of the planet Saturn

> *A drunken reveller holding a skull in his hands.*

Denotes one who is prone to take a fatalistic view of life and to play with it as a cat plays with a
50

GEMINI

mouse. He may perform acts which will cause him suffering and sorrow, and seek to stifle memories in indulgence. Let him transmute himself, and turn his thoughts to the real, fine, and true, and so realize the philosophic power of Saturn when contained in Mercury. It is a symbol of Menace.

♊ 21°. UNDER THE INFLUENCE OF THE PLANET SATURN.

An old man in a graveyard, standing under a cypress-tree, watching a form rising from a tomb.

Denotes one who will be addicted to spiritual phenomena and who will indulge in experiments from which most people would turn away in fear. He will later study closely the higher branches of occult philosophy, for which his peculiar power is well fitted. It is a symbol of Occultism.

♊ 22°. UNDER THE INFLUENCE OF THE PLANET SATURN.

A heap of stones over which ivy is growing.

Denotes one who clings to others for business and advantage, and who will be careful, saving, and given to the accumulation of the riches of the world. He will recognize those useful for his purposes, and recognizing them he will secure

51

them. The symbol is not without its danger and its threatenings. It is a symbol of Clinging.

♊ 23°. UNDER THE INFLUENCE OF THE PLANET URANUS.

> *A triangular-shaped hill. On one side the sun is shining on pleasant paths and beautiful foliage—the other side is dark and gloomy.*

Denotes one who should make the most of his first half of life, when fortune will favour him, and when the happiest and most useful thoughts will reign supreme. The latter part of life promises nothing. It is a path of a peculiar and mysterious nature, and must be approached with caution. He will possess a love of refinement, especially early in life. It is a symbol of Trial.

♊ 24°. UNDER THE INFLUENCE OF THE PLANET URANUS.

> *A beautiful woman giving bread to a crowd of starving people. From behind her, showing dimly through a haze of white light, is a high Intelligence placing a crown of a bright strange metal on her head.*

Denotes one who accounts charity the highest of the virtues—charity of soul, charity of thought, and charity of action. When a generous act is performed, when charity is given to the opinions of others, and in relieving the sufferings of others, when there is unselfishness in act and judgment, the mystic crown bathed in holy light is on the head. It is a symbol of Glory.

♊ 25°. UNDER THE INFLUENCE OF THE PLANET NEPTUNE.

A hand issuing from the heavens holding a great scroll on which is shining a pentagram.

Denotes one of considerable occult force who has a mission to perform and must do what he is destined to do, no matter how strongly he may be opposed. It will be useless for the native to allow himself to be drawn into the world's gambling and money schemes or towards the lower elements of material life. It is a symbol of Etherealism.

♊ 26°. UNDER THE INFLUENCE OF THE PLANET NEPTUNE.

A broken trident falling into the sea.

Denotes one who will be compelled to face uncertain and unsettled conditions. Speculations are fatal to him, and should be avoided. He must exercise care in speech and action, and must not be misled by appearances. It is a symbol of Allurement.

♊ 27°. UNDER THE INFLUENCE OF THE PLANET NEPTUNE.

A man seated at a table, gloomily looking at a violin with broken strings before him.

Denotes one of unsettled firmness who allows the remediable ills in life to affect him. He gives way to worry, anxiety, and gloom without any real cause, for the solution is always at hand if he thinks a little—generally it is in himself. Let him exercise his will, and bring into action his fine understanding. Then will even an instrument with broken strings yield music. It is a symbol of Surrender.

♊ 28°. UNDER THE INFLUENCE OF THE PLANET MARS.

A number of workmen building a railway track through barren country.

Denotes one who through industry and prudence finds ways to aid himself over the greatest difficulties, and in aiding himself he confers lasting benefits on others. He approaches problems with determination and an understanding mind, and

54

grapples until he firmly masters them. It is a symbol of Indefatigableness.

♊ 29°. UNDER THE INFLUENCE OF THE PLANET MARS.

A child blowing a steel glove from a cube of stone.

Denotes one of simplicity of character, gifted with magnetic fire and knowledge of the power of invisible forces. Against him aggression will avail nothing, and the aggressor will find that he himself is conquered. It is a symbol of Seership.

♊ 30°. UNDER THE INFLUENCE OF THE PLANET VENUS.

A maiden bound to a stake smiling at an angel. Near-by lie three dead bats.

Denotes one who is forced by fate to meet many obstacles, dangers, and deceptions, and whose scope of action is limited and held within bounds. The life is a peculiar one, full of threatenings, dangers, strange feelings, incidents, and uncommon action. It is a symbol of Stumbling.

CANCER

♋ 1°. UNDER THE INFLUENCE OF THE PLANET VENUS.

A curious ring set with a large heart of white onyx.

Denotes one of occult learning and of an extremely sensitive and sympathetic nature who will do much for the pleasure and help of the people. He is gifted with a peculiar power, which produces a feeling of calmness and serenity. He may not be free from his own worries, but the power to cast away such poison is his, and he will find that the rays of good he throws out for others will react with added force on himself. It is a symbol of Compassion.

♋ 2°. UNDER THE INFLUENCE OF THE PLANET VENUS.

A labourer leaning against a tree watching a number of others digging in a neighbouring field.

Denotes one who lets others do the work which

he should do for himself. He is fond of the luxuries of life, but is quite content to receive without the toil of gaining them. He can advance his own philosophy to uphold his actions, and will be supported throughout his present life on earth. It is a symbol of Inertia.

♋ 3°.   UNDER THE INFLUENCE OF THE MOON.

A creeping plant—worms eating at the root— growing over a rustic summer-house.

Denotes one who inclines to a quiet and simple life away from the din and struggle of cities. Of a kind and trusting nature, he may leave his vital affairs too much in the hands of others, and thus risk danger, trouble, and losses. He will be wise to look to his affairs and to those he trusts to attend to them. It is a symbol of Entrusting.

♋ 4°.   UNDER THE INFLUENCE OF THE MOON.

A drunken reveller in fancy costume asleep at a table, the contents of his overturned cup of red wine pouring on to the floor.

Denotes a romantic but erratic nature who leads himself to esteem the follies of the world before wisdom. In his pursuit of happiness he will find nothing but exhaustion and fatigue and emptiness. It is a symbol of Misdirection.

♋ 5°. UNDER THE INLFUENCE OF THE SUN.

A man seated on a rock on a newly boomed goldfield, a new pick and shovel beside him, looking gloomily at a newspaper containing reports of rich finds in the locality.

Denotes one who takes too much notice of reports and who ventures before he has obtained enough evidence as to the nature of his speculations. This tendency, unless checked, leads him to a land of famine instead of a land of plenty. It is a symbol of Pitfalls.

♋ 6°. UNDER THE INFLUENCE OF THE SUN.

A man spending money lavishly entertaining his friends, a clown hidden behind a curtain laughing at him.

Denotes one to whom money comes, but who dissipates it, and falls into need again. He must control an extravagant tendency which can only bring him ephemeral friends and leave him but trouble and misery. It is a symbol of Wastefulness.

♋ 7°. UNDER THE INFLUENCE OF THE SUN.

An antique, gold-capped Corinthian column of white marble, slightly crumbling at its base.

Denotes one who strives to stand erect. Time does not cast him down, for grandeur and beauty are his companions ; but beauty, however sublime, is never without a flaw, for the flaw intensifies the beauty. The erect column indicates strength, the crumbling at the base fear, which alone can destroy if permitted to infect the whole. Where faith is, then fear will be never. True faith is knowledge absolute, and what knowledge so perfect as the consciousness in man of his own strength ? It is a symbol of Gracefulness.

♋ 8°. UNDER THE INFLUENCE OF THE PLANET MERCURY.

A newspaper editor at his desk—a mass of proofs before him—parleying with a man who averts his face.

Denotes one whose position in life will enable him to hold many secrets connected with the lives of others and who wields a power which will cause fear to many of position and reputation. A desire for material advantages may cause him to sway in the pursuit of his duty. It is a symbol of Muzzling.

♋ 9°. UNDER THE INFLUENCE OF THE PLANET MERCURY.

An acrobat performing before a large audience.

Denotes one who comes before the public and

59

whose risky adventures secure him favour. He sees many changes in life, and has a hard struggle at times, but his energy and resourcefulness are great, and his spirits never fail. Great wealth will not fall to the native, but his life will not end for lack of means. It is a symbol of Publicity.

♋ 10°.   UNDER THE INFLUENCE OF THE PLANET VENUS.

A painter at his easel in a graceful forest glade. It is the hour of sunset, and strange shadows of unearthly grandeur are falling.

Denotes one of much perseverance and artistic power, to whom the poetry of form and colour appeal most magically. He has a love of quiet, and a rustic life will help to draw to his soul a wealth of inspiration and calm. His search is not for immortality, for this is old knowledge to him. He sees deeply into the imperishable paths, tasting of their everlasting grandeur. It is a symbol of Sublimity.

♋ 11°.   UNDER THE INFLUENCE OF THE PLANET VENUS.

A number of maidens, crowned with garlands of wild flowers, dancing on a green lawn.

Denotes one of bright and joyous spirit and
60

friendly nature whose desire it is to spread happiness and contentment wherever he goes. The native will always be much loved and popular. He comes to the world with a message of love, life, and hope, and a mind which resists the encroachments of evil. It is a symbol of Simplicity.

♋ 12°. UNDER THE INFLUENCE OF THE PLANET VENUS.

An avenue of trees bending before a destructive wind-storm, the rich golden leaves of autumn falling thickly.

Denotes one whose thoughts will be directed to securing a competency for himself in old age, and who will labour hard to accomplish his desire. His love of quiet is disturbed and outraged, and he will be shaken by storms as a tree in the wind. Still he fights on in gloom or sunshine, passing sadness on the way. It is a symbol of Bending.

♋ 13°. UNDER THE INFLUENCE OF THE PLANET MARS.

A volcano in active eruption devastating the country for miles around, whilst groups of peasants cling to their little homes.

Denotes one who is born to face danger and to

61

indulge in undertakings of a venturesome nature which yield little profit and entail much trouble. He is rather fixed in his ideas, and may fail to fall in with the views of the majority. Neither will he attempt to escape when the storm is against him. It is a symbol of Pertinacity.

♋ 14°. UNDER THE INFLUENCE OF THE PLANET MARS.

A crab climbing up an upright iron spear, above which is a circlet of seven stars.

Denotes one who, never daunted by obstacles, opposition, and hardship, will rise by his own effort to a position of dignity and importance in his special sphere. Uniting an iron will to stubbornness of purpose, the native proves his worth, and triumphs. It is a symbol of Irrefragability.

♋ 15°. UNDER THE INFLUENCE OF THE PLANET JUPITER.

An auctioneer's hammer lying on a heap of gold money and bank-notes.

Denotes one who acts with craft and sagacity towards his point of attainment and who will ever struggle hard to hold what he gets. His attitude brings material gain, and his methods bring others

62

under his influence. His life will not be without its disappointments, but he is not the man to yield to " set-backs." His philosophy is self-preservation. It is a symbol of Disregarding.

♋ 16°. UNDER THE INFLUENCE OF THE PLANET JUPITER.

A young man standing on the top of a high mountain, the world stretched out below him, grasping a sword which comes from the heavens to his hand.

Denotes one who is entrusted with a high mission and who is deeply inspired, having a spirituality entirely serene. To him has the mandate " Go forth and teach the people " been echoed from the heavens. He will be granted power and influence, so that the people will hear him call. The evidences of this peculiar mission are made manifest in his twelfth year and mature between the twenty-fourth and thirty-sixth years. It is the symbol of the Inspired.

♋ 17°. UNDER THE INFLUENCE OF THE PLANET JUPITER.

A band of merchants on camels travelling through the wilderness.

Denotes a lover of travelling whose leanings are

63

towards a nomadic life. He is, however, keenly alive to the necessity of material work, and he traffics in stuffs the sale of which is not confined to any one district or country. He will accumulate by or through merchandise, exporting and importing, or through things of universal demand. Sometimes indiscreet, sometimes hasty, the native is always self-possessed. It is a symbol of Exchanging.

♋ 18°. UNDER THE INFLUENCE OF THE PLANET SATURN.

A hand grasping gold pieces, some of which are falling through the fingers.

Denotes one who is disposed to place too much value on material things, esteeming them as philosophy and learning, one who will make his days " pay " him, and who seeks to gain the wealth of the world by all legitimate means. His nature is somewhat hard ; he regards " his best friends, the friends of his pocket," hence does not know his truest friends at all. He will continue thus to the end of his earth days, when, as the Talmud has it, " all that he has gained slips through his fingers." It is a symbol of Materialism.

CANCER

♋ 19°. UNDER THE INFLUENCE OF THE PLANET SATURN.

An old man sitting alone in semi-darkness with an old book before him, from which emanate bright rays of light.

Denotes one whose whole life is devoted to finding out truth which gives him certainty beyond mere belief. He will never be daunted in his search, no matter how the storms drive round him. As the All-Divine Designer of the Grand Design draws his earth days to a close, he sees the Darling of his pilgrimage face to face, and seeing knows. It is a symbol of Essentials.

♋ 20°. UNDER THE INFLUENCE OF THE PLANET URANUS.

A wounded Bedouin mounted on his horse in the desert.

Denotes one of unsettled tendencies with a strong desire for freedom and liberty of movement who, brave, daring, and adventurous, is ever restless if held to one place for long. He is not well fitted for ordinary life, as his employment changes so much, and some of these changes will be sudden. His nature is wilful, erratic, impulsive, and his body is marked naturally or by accident. It is a symbol of Liberty.

♋ 21°. UNDER THE INFLUENCE OF THE PLANET URANUS.

A man having jumped over a fence falls into a ditch on the other side of it.

Denotes one who is overventuresome and liable to fall into grave mistakes and errors. He should be exceedingly careful of his conduct and endeavour by strength of will to moderate an impulsiveness which if allowed to grow will bring into form all the threatenings of this peculiar degree. Self-mastery and the forcing of self to obey the power of his spirit should be his chief care in life. It is a symbol of Hastiness.

♋ 22°. UNDER THE INFLUENCE OF THE PLANET URANUS.

A jewelled crown falling from a height into mud.

Denotes one whose life will have a powerful influence on the people—one who rises to power through no special virtue of his own and who as a consequence of a false education and evil impressions uses his influence badly, going down to a hopeless grave. It is a symbol of Extinction.

♋ 23°. UNDER THE INFLUENCE OF THE PLANET NEPTUNE.

Fishermen pulling in their nets in calm weather.

Denotes one whose business in life is uncertain

in its results, but who can calmly go on, contented to take whatever fate sends his way. He is gifted with mediumistic power and his impressions enable him to make but few mistakes in his affairs. It is a symbol of Peacefulness.

♋ 24°. UNDER THE INFLUENCE OF THE PLANET NEPTUNE.

A graceful dancer smilingly receiving applause and floral tributes.

Denotes one of charming manners and graceful style, poetic and artistic, who will be a general favourite. He is fortunate in an artistic or professional career or any calling which brings him in direct touch with the public. The infant life is threatened and should be guarded. It is a symbol of Pleasing.

♋ 25°. UNDER THE INFLUENCE OF THE PLANET MARS.

The setting Sun reflected from the sea in such a manner that the reflected rays interlace with the solar rays.

Denotes a psychic readily absorbing the thoughts and suggestions of others. He should never permit himself to be hypnotized nor entranced, nor give way to negative states of mind or lowering

67

thoughts. He must absorb noble teachings and eschew unworthy ones. Then as he reaches the latter part of his earth life glories will stream from his soul to unite with the lights of the heaven of aspiration. It is a symbol of Impressions.

♋ 26°. UNDER THE INFLUENCE OF THE PLANET MARS.

A marksman having failed to hit the bull's-eye in eight shots strikes it in the ninth.

Denotes one of a persevering spirit who is not disposed to sink under failures be they ever so frequent, nor will argument turn his mind from a set purpose, for in his soul is the knowledge that success will come to him in the end. In his attempts he is orderly, never undertaking a new thing before he has finished that which he has in hand. It is a symbol of the Undaunted.

♋ 27°. UNDER THE INFLUENCE OF THE PLANET MARS.

A moth circling round a flame.

Denotes one who can be hypnotized by glitter and glare, power and show, and who takes risks which less impulsive people would shrink from. The will is too yielding and the love of pleasure too great. Let him remember that the moth

68

which circles round the flame is ultimately drawn into it and consumed, and that the death of the moth does not trouble the flame. It is a symbol of Glitter.

♋ 28°.   UNDER THE INFLUENCE OF THE PLANET VENUS.

An old mill-wheel lying on the bank of a lily pond, with pretty creepers growing over it.

Denotes one whose life will be peaceful and whose marriage will be blessed. His desires are simple and his talents are natural. He does not wish to rule in the world of men. His mental attitude and manner of living form a magnetic point of help and sympathy where the world-worn may have balm for their wounds. It is a symbol of Charm.

♋ 29°.   UNDER THE INFLUENCE OF THE PLANET VENUS.

A man in a prison cell, a ray of light flowing through the bars, on which a little bird stands singing.

Denotes one liable to be bound soul and body, who will be restricted in action and desire. But even so he may yet release his true self and meet the force flowing from the fountain head. Thus,

69

though one side may frown and obstruct him, the other will smile and release him. It is a symbol of Obstruction.

♋ 30°. UNDER THE INFLUENCE OF THE PLANET MERCURY.

A winged wheel flying across a green field.

Denotes one of character, force, and skill who by the hand of destiny will rise to a position in this world in which he is fitted to play a decided part. He has a keen imagination and considerable constructive ability. He gains from travelling and change. It is a symbol of Continuance.

LEO

♌

♌ 1°. UNDER THE INFLUENCE OF THE PLANET MERCURY.

A king stepping from his carriage receiving a document from a group of citizens.

Denotes one who will be enabled to grant or to refuse to grant the wishes of others. He will reach a position of importance and will receive many honours, and benefits will accrue to him. The demand is for an understanding of the use, not the abuse, of power. It is a symbol of Authority.

♌ 2°. UNDER THE INFLUENCE OF THE PLANET MERCURY.

A roll of papers having dropped from the hand of a dying scholar is eagerly caught up by an eminent professor on whose face there is a look of triumph.

Denotes one whose early life is threatened and who in later years will gain possession of material

71

secrets discovered by another which he has long sought to obtain. Having obtained them, he claims the discoveries as his own, gaining thus further professional advancement and reputation. His triumph may last till he breathes his last breath, then he will learn what in spite of all his learning he does not know, and his action of yesterday brings remorse on the morrow. It is a symbol of Artifice.

♌ 3°.   UNDER THE INFLUENCE OF THE SUN.

A huge human head. From the left eye emanates a ray of black vapour, from the right a ray of yellow, and from the centre of the forehead a ray of white.

Denotes a remarkable personality who has an understanding of complex subjects. Rich, courted, and strong, he can regulate his forces for the blessing or bane of men. There is also an entirely occult side to this symbol which expresses the same meaning from a spiritual outlook. It is a symbol of Leadership.

♌ 4°.   UNDER THE INFLUENCE OF THE SUN.

An ambassador leaving the presence of a prince who is smiling significantly to his chancellor.

Denotes one who may be deceived by smiles and

promises. He should be especially careful of those in power, and should be wary lest in negotiations he betrays his plans and aspirations to keen and subtle adversaries. Wisdom is in silence. It is a symbol of Treachery.

♌ 5°. UNDER THE INFLUENCE OF THE PLANET MERCURY.

A lawyer placing a document before a client, who signs it. His eyes are bandaged.

Denotes one who should be critically careful of attaching his name to papers and in putting absolute trust in interested advisers. In all writings, care should be taken if the native would save himself sorrow, suffering, and the results of impulsive action. He should look many times at a pen before he dips it in the ink. It is a symbol of Complications.

♌ 6°. UNDER THE INFLUENCE OF THE PLANET MERCURY.

A lion crouching in a jungle with a large bird of the eagle type in his mouth.

Denotes one who will be compelled to fight and struggle during a great part of his life and who will often have to use his ingenuity to release himself from entanglements and troubles. He

73

may have financial difficulties or difficulties over property or estates. In the end—perhaps even in the midst of worry—his star rises and he triumphs over enemies and evil conditions. It is a symbol of Strategy.

♌ 7°. UNDER THE INFLUENCE OF THE PLANET MERCURY.

A book, on which is a crown, resting on a golden throne.

Denotes one who will by his own skill and ability receive and profit by impressions and reach a position which gains him the recognition due to him. To such, perseverance and faith are the essentials, and if he regards the meaning of these two words apart from the words themselves he will crown his labours with success. It is a symbol of Fame.

♌ 8°. UNDER THE INFLUENCE OF THE PLANET VENUS.

Two lovers walking in a forest glade. Before them are two doves and a brilliantly coloured butterfly.

Denotes one of an idealistic and affectionate disposition whose poetic nature will at times put him out of touch with the world of men, its false

74

ideas of justice, and its oceans of pain. Then
should he "seek the forest lands for peace and
heaven." He is himself a happy influence and
generally he will be favoured. Should the horoscope show marriage it will be a union of souls.
It is a symbol of Affection.

♌ 9°. UNDER THE INFLUENCE OF THE PLANET
VENUS.

*A lady, elegantly dressed and bedecked with
many jewels, standing before a mirror.*

Denotes one fortunate, but somewhat vain, whose
desire it is " to make a good appearance " and
who expends much money for this purpose. But
the glories which shine forth from a great soul
glitter more than the choicest diamond in the
daintiest setting, giving a lasting beauty which
age cannot change nor time obliterate. There are
two sides to this symbol, and both reflect, for it
is a symbol of Reflection.

♌ 10°. UNDER THE INFLUENCE OF THE PLANET
MARS.

*A soldier rescuing a wounded comrade on a
field of battle—a dark, sinister figure rising
behind him.*

Denotes one of brave, fearless, and noble disposition whose natural greatness of soul is moved by the necessities of others, and who always puts the well-being of another before his own comforts. Envy is directed against him and malice turns her evil eyes on him. He will be exposed to many and grave dangers, for duty to him is ever the first thought. It is a symbol of Daring.

♌ 11°. UNDER THE INFLUENCE OF THE PLANET MARS.

A troop of old barbarian soldiers carrying off struggling women.

Denotes one over whom the wild senses strive for mastery, whose philosophy of force crumbles before what is truly real. The time may come when he will be forced to pause, when he will be made to see the uselessness of it all, and how strangely things are mirrored in the world of illusion. He must strive lest he become the slave of his lower self and the inducer of his own dangers. It is a symbol of Indulgence.

♌ 12°. UNDER THE INFLUENCE OF THE PLANET MARS.

A man of martial and distinguished bearing giving alms to the poor.

Denotes one of brave and generous disposition
76

who is an earnest and sincere champion of the oppressed and who is one of that great band who cannot be deaf to the moans of the suffering many. He is a militant, generous force, and in his philosophy " charity covereth a multitude of sins." It is a symbol of Humanity.

♌ 13°. UNDER THE INFLUENCE OF THE PLANET JUPITER.

An old oak-tree over which shines the noon-day sun in a clear sky.

Denotes one of rugged, conservative, and patriotic nature who will be blessed with the goods of the world and who will use his blessings well. His position in life will be distinguished and his sincerity will command respect even from his enemies. He carries about him a fine and pure aura which benefits all who come within its radiations. It is a symbol of Exaltation.

♌ 14°. UNDER THE INFLUENCE OF THE PLANET JUPITER.

Two men tossing coins whilst another looks on.

Denotes one of a sporting nature whose instincts are keenly set on those things which the world is content to regard as chance happenings. The native will not be greatly interested in chance as a problem amenable to scientific treatment. He prefers to ever regard it as the absolute unknown and to let its solution be a matter of risk. It is a symbol of Gaming.

♌ 15°. UNDER THE INFLUENCE OF THE PLANET SATURN.

A mass of black rock in the centre of which is a large diamond.

Denotes one who is forced to labour hard for the greater part of his life, but who contains within himself some brilliant gifts, one of which will progress and bring him into fame. It is a symbol of Creeping.

♌ 16°. UNDER THE INFLUENCE OF THE PLANET SATURN.

A pyramid in the midst of a sand waste, with lowering black clouds above it.

Denotes one who in the midst of threats, difficulties, and oppositions raises himself to a position of dignity and responsibility, and the stings of envy will follow him. He will see many pass through this world of matter before he receives the call, and will keenly feel and deplore his errors. He may find that the road to power is not the road to happiness. It is a symbol of Vexation.

78

LEO

♌ 17°. UNDER THE INFLUENCE OF THE PLANET SATURN.

An architect standing by a desk with the plans of a building before him.

Denotes one of understanding and power of purpose who is gifted with fine perception and a lively imagination.   As a theorist he is generally correct in his deductions and he can quickly clothe his thoughts in material dress.   It is a symbol of Knowledge.

♌ 18°. UNDER THE INFLUENCE OF THE PLANET URANUS.

Two gold-miners seated near mining machinery examining a strange metal unknown to modern science, which they have found amongst the quartz.

Denotes one of a peculiar and original mind with a strong leaning towards the unravelling of the many mysteries of science.   Entirely unorthodox in his methods of research, he is not likely to obtain recognition from book-drilled students, but people of true learning will always be attracted to him.   The personality is double, and he is able to carry on two lines of investigation at the same time.   It is a symbol of Introspection.

♌ 19°.　UNDER THE INFLUENCE OF THE PLANET
URANUS.

*A giant holding a number of bleeding hearts
pierced on his sword.*

Denotes a man of compelling will and magnetic
force who stops at nothing to carry out his
ambitions. He rises to power through blood or
tears or both. He wields and binds, and those
whom he binds will bleed, for his work is the
work of materialistic pride which dissolves in the
fires of hate. It is a symbol of Compulsion.

♌ 20°.　UNDER THE INFLUENCE OF THE PLANET
NEPTUNE.

A violin and bow lying on some sheets of music.

Denotes one of a refined and harmonious nature,
skilful in one of the entertaining arts, and a
psychic of some ability. He is gifted as a composer either of music or some allied art. It is
a symbol of Refinement.

♌ 21°.　UNDER THE INFLUENCE OF THE PLANET
NEPTUNE.

*A man in the robes of a magician tracing
mystic signs on the sands of the seashore in
the silence of night.*

Denotes one of mystical mind who is attracted

to the ritualistic and ceremonial. The mind is capable of serious thought, seeing miracles in actions which to others seem quite commonplace. With him romance, poetry, and wonderment travel. It is a symbol of Mysticism.

♌ 22°. UNDER THE INFLUENCE OF THE PLANET NEPTUNE.

A man carrying a bird in a golden cage.

Denotes one who is in danger of being held in restraint of some kind and of being moved to different places at the will of others. There is no suggestion of unkind treatment, but there is that the native is not a free agent. He should never permit others to gain an influence over him in any way. He is very mediumistic, but can be controlled from the visible as he can from the invisible. It is a symbol of Restriction.

♌ 23°. UNDER THE INFLUENCE OF THE PLANET MARS.

A trumpet made from a ram's horn bathed in the sun's rays.

Denotes a rouser of men, one destined for action, who will bring light and benefit to mankind. His way will not be without its roughness, and many times he will be weary. Then the sound

81

of the horn will rouse him to an understanding of his work and he will see the light.   It is a symbol of Incitement.

♌ 24°.   UNDER THE INFLUENCE OF THE PLANET MARS.

An old rusty sword, over which grass is growing, outside a rustic cottage.

Denotes one who, after struggling and fighting to gain ascendancy in the world of illusion, realizes in his later life the futility of it all, and throwing away his aggressive sword he retires to a life of peace and simplicity, whilst the sword rots to decay and the tender grass covers it as the flowers over a grave.   It is a symbol of Renunciation.

♌ 25°.   UNDER THE INFLUENCE OF THE PLANET VENUS.

A poet reading his verses to a group of ladies in an old castle garden.

Denotes one whose influence will be ideal and cultivating, and who, notwithstanding his simplicity of character, is not without a degree of pride.   This alloy but serves to show the points of artistic excellence, and will not prejudice him if kept within bounds.   It is a symbol of Proportion.

82

LEO

♌ 26°. UNDER THE INFLUENCE OF THE PLANET VENUS.

Two hands clasped under a floral crown.

Denotes one talented, poetic, and scientific who gains much through the quiet influence of helpful friends. He himself is true and peaceful. He dislikes quarrels and disturbed conditions. He is considerate in his dealings with others, and can be relied on to keep a secret. It is a symbol of Comradeship.

♌ 27°. UNDER THE INFLUENCE OF THE PLANET VENUS.

A bleeding hand holding a thorny orange branch on which the fruit is growing.

Denotes one who will be compelled to gain experience through suffering, losses, and deceit. He is sincere and affectionate, and will sacrifice much to help another. He is aided, patronized, and advanced, and from his former sufferings his fame springs. It is a symbol of Approval.

♌ 28°. UNDER THE INFLUENCE OF THE PLANET MERCURY.

A stream of oil falling from mid-air upon the troubled waters beneath.

Denotes one who will exercise discrimination in

83

the affairs of daily life ; one who will possess tact, understanding, and diplomacy, and a peculiar magnetic aura which enables him to bring quarrelling units to a peaceful union. It is a symbol of Conciliation.

♌ 29°. UNDER THE INFLUENCE OF THE PLANET MERCURY.

A man climbing a ladder and helping others who strive behind him. At the top, a veiled figure holds out to him a wreath of stars.

Denotes one who has power enough to rise in the world and heart enough to help others to rise. *His* destiny *is* to rise. It is his soul of sympathy and justice which merits the victor's wreath, and his every action of kindness to the struggling and to the suffering brings to him blessings of power, adding heavenly glory to the rewards awaiting him. It is a symbol of Rewarding.

♌ 30°. UNDER THE INFLUENCE OF THE MOON.

A ship's steward carrying a bowl of enchanting white lilies.

Denotes a changeable person, loving to journey about. He gains much benefit from ships, shipping, means of transit, and the public. While on a journey he meets his greatest happiness. He is generally fortunate with his friends and in all his affairs of life. It is a symbol of Voyaging.

*

VIRGO

♍

♍ 1°. Under the influence of the moon.

A travelling pilgrim leaning on his staff, which he holds in his left hand, addressing a small band of men and women.

Denotes one whose early life is threatened by the elements and who will be compelled to endure sufferings, hardships, and trials as an atonement for remote past acts. If his destiny is to live, his destiny is to overcome, and he will be a wise instructor and guide to his fellow-men. It is a symbol of Repaying.

♍ 2°. Under the influence of the moon.

A waning moon in a sky, half of which is clear and studded with stars, and half of which is covered with dark clouds which herald an approaching storm.

Denotes one of considerable ability who, as his life grows older, will be plunged into difficulties and trouble.   It is well for one born in this degree

to study his actions and to be scrupulously
cautious as to his plans and movements. He
should avoid speculative ventures, guard against
deceit and treachery, and do all that is possible
to lead an even, temperate life. It is a symbol of
Threatenings.

♍ 3°. UNDER THE INFLUENCE OF THE PLANET
MERCURY.

*A young woman working at a spinning-wheel
by a cottage window, which opens on a smiling
garden in which bees are flying amongst the
flowers.*

Denotes one who is gifted with a sunny nature,
patience, and the ability to labour hard and to
endure. He will produce works of benefit and
charm, and experience will expand his soul and
teach him the truth which he values as a com-
panion to beauty. It is a symbol of Persistency.

♍ 4°. UNDER THE INFLUENCE OF THE PLANET
MERCURY.

*A bookbinder fastening covers on a number of
unbound books.*

Denotes one who spreads knowledge of some
special nature whose position in life will be one
of trust and responsibility. His mind is analytical

and exact, and his actions are regulated by necessity and the acts of others. " Safe bind, safe find," is his motto, and carelessness does not enter into his nature. It is a symbol of Protecting.

♍ 5°. UNDER THE INFLUENCE OF THE PLANET VENUS.

An artist working at a large piece of tapestry of charming design, which he has almost completed.

Denotes one of a constructive and artistic mind, a lover of art, and quaint but picturesque philosophies ; one who perceives the exquisite loveliness of an old garden, a moss-covered wall, a running brook, and nature's changing moods, and who is attracted to old-world lores. It is a symbol of Conservatism.

♍ 6°. UNDER THE INFLUENCE OF THE PLANET VENUS.

A large ballroom in which men and women are dancing.

Denotes one of light and free mind who allows nothing to oppress him. He meets with favours and enjoys gifts. He loves the beautiful in form and colour. Scents and perfumes fascinate him. It is a symbol of Elegance.

VIRGO

♍ 7°. UNDER THE INFLUENCE OF THE PLANET VENUS.

A man in ceremonial robes, with a circlet about his brow, holding the emblem of life—the Crux ansata—in the air.

Denotes one who finds in the philosophies of the ancient masters the true knowledge of life, whose search for the truth is rewarded, and who, in consequence of his dread of doing wrong, has the power of drawing the greatness of right towards him. It is a symbol of Philosophy.

♍ 8°. UNDER THE INFLUENCE OF THE PLANET MARS.

A man, holding a pen in his right hand and a sword in his left, standing at the entrance to a palace.

Denotes one of forceful and aggressive mind who presses onwards with energy and determination. His assertiveness will not easily be opposed, and in all his dealings with others he demands the answer to be " Yes " or " No," for to his mind there is no middle course. He will draw to himself great responsibilities and will ever be involved in argument and dispute. It is a symbol of Assertion.

ZODIACAL SYMBOLOGY

♍ 9°. UNDER THE INFLUENCE OF THE PLANET MARS.

A sack of corn, from a hole in which the grain is falling out.

Denotes one who through neglect and want of caution is likely to risk too much. To him speculation and gambling will only mean gradual ruin. He should be careful of his associations and dealings with other people, of his business transactions, and his manner of life. It is a symbol of Carelessness.

♍ 10°. UNDER THE INFLUENCE OF THE PLANET JUPITER.

A sibyl in a cave, seated on a tripod beneath which is a cloud of smoke. The leaves of fate are flying into the open air through the mouth of the cavern.

Denotes one of a fatalistic mind who sees in the operations of nature, the actions of men, the habits of animals, and the growth of plants the direct manifestations of the Divine Mind ; and who holds that what is laid down must ever be, for the Will of God cannot be changed, and man and nature are but allies in the fulfilment of it. It is a symbol of Fatalism.

90

♍ 11°.   UNDER THE INFLUENCE OF THE PLANET
JUPITER.

> *A king, seated in a chariot drawn by two stags,*
> *throwing coins to some peasants who are singing*
> *on the roadside.*

Denotes one who is born to honour and who will
be esteemed for his goodness of heart and appreciation of effort.   The position he gains by
perseverance will enable him to do well for the
world in many ways.   He receives more than he
gives, and for all he gives he receives blessings
which carry to him a strong and subtle spiritual
force which clings to him for eternity, whilst
what he has given mixes with the elements.   It
is a symbol of Charity.

♍ 12°.   UNDER THE INFLUENCE OF THE PLANET
JUPITER.

> *A horseman holding with difficulty a rearing*
> *horse.*

Denotes one who is drawn into rash ventures
and who will be forced to work hard to save
those things truly his own.   He may be too
dependent on his strength, which he overtaxes,
or on his resources, which he overstrains.   The
rising planet contains the warning.   It is a symbol
of Grappling.

♍ 13°.   UNDER THE INFLUENCE OF THE PLANET
SATURN.

*A large black cloud, around which are bright
silver lights.*

Denotes one who will endure much sorrow and
strange experiences. He is well and strangely
gifted, and will leave his mark on the world.
He should be cautious in his choice of companions, and should not allow fading, falling
allurements to threaten him on the way. It is
a symbol of Tribulation.

♍ 14°.   UNDER THE INFLUENCE OF THE PLANET
SATURN.

*A torn document, old and crinkled, on which
is a large black seal.*

Denotes one of a conservative and old-world mind
who talks little, but to the point. He will be
out of touch with modern society, leaning neither
to their teachings nor ideals. He will have
struggles and hard climbs, and does not think
enough of possessions ever to become wealthy.
He holds what he possesses and lives quietly.
It is a symbol of Conscientiousness.

VIRGO

♍ 15°. UNDER THE INFLUENCE OF THE PLANET
URANUS.

> *A radiant rainbow, in the centre of which is
> the sun in its brightness.*

Denotes a lover of nature in her grandeur, one of
artistic, mystic, and philosophic mind, who will
move about a great deal and travel to various
places. He is capable of spreading the light of
truth and of helping many to see and appreciate
its marvels. This degree is a fortunate one and
promises much. It is a symbol of Arising.

♍ 16°. UNDER THE INFLUENCE OF THE PLANET
URANUS.

> *A fire emitting flames of beautiful colour-blends.*

Denotes a thinker of thoughts, but slightly
regarded by the mass of present-day earth men,
who seeks for right, feeling the silent appeal of
beauty and the cry of oppressed humanity. His
is a deep, sensitive nature—poetic, romantic, and
full of action. It is a symbol of Luminosity.

♍ 17°. UNDER THE INFLUENCE OF THE PLANET
URANUS.

> *An astrologer seated at a desk, his head resting
> on his left hand, judging a nativity.*

Denotes a student of the prophetic and curious

93

arts who will command respect, one of skilled judgment and dignified bearing, devoid of pride and littleness. He will prove a trusted guide, especially to the masses, from whom he benefits. It is a symbol of Foreknowing.

♍ 18°.   UNDER THE INFLUENCE OF THE PLANET NEPTUNE.

> *A man, supporting a little girl, swimming towards the shore in a rough sea.*

Denotes one whose mission it is to serve his fellow-men.   He will perform acts which will win him approval and honour.   Life will not be always smooth with him, and he will have his part of sorrow and pain in this world of matter ; but ever near him are the protecting forces, and he cannot fail, no matter how fierce the waves.   It is a symbol of Serving.

♍ 19°.   UNDER THE INFLUENCE OF THE PLANET NEPTUNE.

> *A rough fire mountain, from several parts of which smoke is rising. On one of the slopes labourers are working.*

Denotes one who exercises patience and persistence in his life's work, and whose position is oft attended with much worry and personal danger.

VIRGO

His soul is full of enterprise. He is magnetic, psychic, and extremely active. It is a symbol of Endeavour.

♍ 20°. UNDER THE INFLUENCE OF THE PLANET MARS.

A great grey warship with her decks cleared ready for action.

Denotes one of pugnacious nature who forces his demands and ideas by sheer power of mind. He has strong magnetic force and knows when to use it. He travels much in search of adventure and gain, and holds the fruits of his labours. It is a symbol of Purpose.

♍ 21°. UNDER THE INFLUENCE OF THE PLANET MARS.

A man burning a will as he triumphantly looks towards another lying on a table.

Denotes one of resourcefulness and determination who can be trusted to protect and safeguard his vital interests. Others, perhaps even amongst his own kinsmen, may interfere or attempt to interfere with the liberty of the native and prevent his free actions, and he may have to use craft to protect his rights and himself. It is a symbol of Finesse.

♍ 22°. UNDER THE INFLUENCE OF THE PLANET MARS.

Nymphs and fauns in the midst of Bacchanalian orgies in the woods.

Denotes one of an artistic and sensuous nature who may be misled by the allurement of passion and desire. He is always a true friend, but may put his trust in the hands of those who are unworthy to hold it. He should be careful lest the awakening brings suffering. Under certain horoscopical conditions this degree can denote one of an entirely opposite nature, but with it there is always some degree of binding. It is a symbol of Seduction.

♍ 23°. UNDER THE INFLUENCE OF THE PLANET VENUS.

The Virgin Astræa, with bandaged eyes, being led away by the angels from the world flooded with blood, misery, injustice, and crime.

Denotes one of a refined and sweet nature who keenly feels the wickedness of this wrongly taught world, which would be God's own paradise were men fair and kind to one another. The native should not allow others to lead him into speculation or any form of gambling or chance. He is ideal in thought, and seer enough to see what might have been. It is a symbol of Sympathy.

♍ 24°. UNDER THE INFLUENCE OF THE PLANET VENUS.

A colossal giant holding a woman in his hand.

Denotes one who may become vain of his earthly power and may use it for purposes which can be of no *real* benefit to him and no *real* gratification. Suffering may force him to hold himself in check and to understand that " he who conquers himself is greater than he who conquers a kingdom." It is a symbol of Violence.

♍ 25°. UNDER THE INFLUENCE OF THE PLANET MERCURY.

A man, from whose forehead streams a dazzling white light, passing through a fiery valley, at the end of which are beautiful lawns, flowers, and trees bathed in brilliant sunlight.

Denotes one of an affectionate, hopeful, and sincere nature who endeavours to do by love alone what others are attempting to do by force. Gifted with a will of strength, he is able to resist and subdue all the demons which rise against him ; thus is his spiritual nature uplifted, and he is inspired and helped from occult sources. He will have struggles in life and difficulties which seem insurmountable, but he *knows* he will overcome them, and he overcomes them all, for they are but sent to teach him what world-life is and what it may be.   It is a symbol of Overcoming.

♍ 26°.   UNDER THE INFLUENCE OF THE PLANET MERCURY.

> *An antique temple of the Muses built on a rock, over which flows an enchanting fall of clear sparkling water.*

Denotes one who would seek the ideal in all things, even amidst the hell of war and the fires of destruction.   One of a strange, happy, though wise philosophy of thought.   He is a votary of art, music, culture, and all uplifting studies.   It is a symbol of Cultivation.

♍ 27°.   UNDER THE INFLUENCE OF THE PLANET MERCURY.

> *A newspaper critic seated in a theatre watching a performance.*

Denotes one of a quick and critical mind who is gifted with powers of observation and discrimination   He is able to turn points to his advantage, and does not hesitate to push forward with energy

98

and activity to gain his desires. It is a symbol of Keenness.

♍ 28°. UNDER THE INFLUENCE OF THE MOON.

A gang of stevedores loading a vessel with product.

Denotes one who works hard and denies himself much. He is entrusted with delicate missions and satisfactory commissions. Work to him is prayer, and he never grumbles at its demands. It is a symbol of Labour.

♍ 29°. UNDER THE INFLUENCE OF THE MOON.

A crescent moon shining with especial brightness in a blue, star-crowded sky.

Denotes one of some especial genius and extremely artistic who is restless under restraint and who loves to roam about. He roams for a purpose and not for idle pleasure, for this native never idles. He has great faith and obtains recognition and success. It is a symbol of Brightness.

♍ 30°. UNDER THE INFLUENCE OF THE SUN.

A heap of bright yellow oranges blown from the tree by the wind.

Denotes one who suffers much deceit and whose hopes are threatened. Himself of a sincere and spiritual nature, he dislikes to find fault with the actions of others, and he goes his own way whether they hurt him or no. Fate is strong in his life, and he is forced by circumstances to accept its ruling. It is a symbol of Circumstances.

LIBRA

♎ 1°. Under the influence of the sun.

A lion with his paw on a heart, above a square.

Denotes one of a highly magnetic and affectionate disposition combined with mental firmness and endurance. The life will be filled with strange happenings, obstacles, and sorrows. The affairs of his heart bring bitterness, but sweetness may come from pain. It is a symbol of Thwarting.

♎ 2°. Under the influence of the sun.

A gold-covered book, on which is cut a Crux ansata crowned, floating in the misty air

Denotes one of psychic understanding, peculiar knowledge, and inspiration, who will produce work of use or distinct beauty. Particularly is his understanding directed to certain knowledge of the continuity of life, especially as regards individual existence. Within himself rages the eternal contest between spirit and matter. At one time matter is triumphant, at another spirit,

101

but spirit will gain in the end.   It is a symbol of Foreseeing.

♎ 3°.   UNDER THE INFLUENCE OF THE PLANET VENUS.

A young girl striving to escape from immaterial, but visible, cords which surround her ; the more she struggles the more they increase.

Denotes one who is in danger of being drawn into psychic conditions from which escape is difficult. Such a one should refrain from dabbling in matters he does not thoroughly understand. Danger in connexion with occult or psychic matters is threatened and much suffering therefrom.   Love affairs may embarrass, especially if intertwined with occult practices.   The native will be gifted in some branch of art or science, but there is a peculiar force fighting against his success and against which a calm placidity is the only protection.   It is a symbol of Involving.

♎ 4°.   UNDER THE INFLUENCE OF THE PLANET VENUS.

A broken wedding-ring lying on a table.

Denotes one whose path will be filled with bitterness, whose affections are enduring, but lacking in the principle of true love.   He is fated to suffer in

102

order to attain development and mind expansion, for his mistakes are many. The experiences of the native will force him to understand the purpose of life. It is a symbol of Isolation.

♎ 5°. UNDER THE INFLUENCE OF THE PLANET MARS.

A naked arm and hand, from which blood is flowing. Above, a sword.

Denotes one who attains influence and a degree of power through aggression, forcefulness, and fighting. He is of an adventurous nature and endures a wound for the glory of getting it and the honour it gains him, and he will have many wounds. It is a symbol of Encroachment.

♎ 6°. UNDER THE INFLUENCE OF THE PLANET MARS.

A traction engine travelling along a newly made road in very charming country.

Denotes one of an artistic nature and a plodding but powerful disposition who is called to do work of a pioneering nature. He is an advocate of force, and the discipline with which he has been bended he would use on others. It is a symbol Pioneering.

≏ 7°. UNDER THE INFLUENCE OF THE PLANET MARS.

A winged globe on the back of a sporting dolphin.

Denotes one with a great message who will travel everywhere and whose thoughts and feelings are expanded and uplifted thereby. His wanderings are often directed beyond this earth to the heavenly fields and to the lands closed to those held in material bodies. He is capable of performing many good acts for others and is ever ready to resist actions unworthy of a true man, holding meanness in contempt. It is a symbol of Movement.

≏ 8°. UNDER THE INFLUENCE OF THE PLANET JUPITER.

A group of people standing dejectedly outside the closed doors of a big financial institution.

Denotes one who will have need to exercise very great caution as to the safe keeping of his worldly possessions. Such a one should keep away from speculations, ventures, and crafty people, and undertake nothing of a nature involving risk. It is a symbol of Forfeiting.

LIBRA

♎ **9°.** UNDER THE INFLUENCE OF THE PLANET
JUPITER.

*A large pair of scales. Two men quarrelling
behind.*

Denotes one who should avoid law and disputes.
Inharmony is to him a state of evil which forces
him into a groove of fate and holds him in bondage.
He should endeavour by the power of his soul
to keep the scales even and do nothing to prejudice
his peace. It is a symbol of Unevenness.

♎ **10°.** UNDER THE INFLUENCE OF THE PLANET
SATURN.

An old hermit, in a cave, grasping a crucifix.

Denotes one of a conservative and religious mind
who is drawn towards solitude. He has many
troubles, and endures mortification and suffering,
but he directs his thoughts to the grand ideal
which materializes as life advances, and this to
him is happiness. It is a symbol of Solitude.

♎ **11°.** UNDER THE INFLUENCE OF THE PLANET
SATURN.

A crow with a large rat in its beak.

Denotes one who is liable to be assailed by
powerful enemies, but who, being conscious of his
own strength, is content to wait patiently until

by frequent attacks they fall at last into his power. He is gifted with patience and sagacity, under- standing and diplomacy. It is a symbol of Defiance.

♎ 12°. UNDER THE INFLUENCE OF THE PLANET SATURN.

A man falling from an insecure and broken bridge into a dark pit below.

Denotes one who will suffer chiefly from a lack of confidence in self and ability to realize his own powers and limitations. Evils may assail his health or financial position, and place him in positions of danger from which he can only escape by the power of a resisting will.   It is a symbol of Timidity.

♎ 13°. UNDER THE INFLUENCE OF THE PLANET URANUS.

A woman in a dark blue costume entering a convent door ; her head is erect, her arms raised, and she heeds not a handsome cavalier who is offering her fruits and flowers.

Denotes one of a refined and highly sensitive nature, religious and disposed to self-immolation. He will be blessed with worldly gifts, but will in the midway of his life know how *really* weak
106

worldly wealth is, and how impotent to satisfy the cravings of the spirit. It is a symbol of Abdication.

≏ 14°.   UNDER THE INFLUENCE OF THE PLANET URANUS.

A brilliantly plumaged peacock strutting towards a wall, behind which are two men unwinding a net.

Denotes one who if not born into worldly wealth will obtain it in another way.   He will have much " good luck " and in consequence will feel unduly elated and proud.   Then is it that danger is near.   He may be snared into a false investment and lose in a night all he has gained in years. It is a symbol of Snaring.

≏ 15°.   UNDER THE INFLUENCE OF THE PLANET NEPTUNE.

A man who has just left the banquet table in a dazed condition, holding his hand to his head as if trying to remember something.

Denotes one who is too psychic for strong drink and strong food, which throw him off his balance and injure the fine machinery of his extremely sensitive brain.   It is when hurt by any form of overindulgence that he renders himself liable

107

to obsession or evil suggestion. If he resists
these evils his gifts will manifest and bring him
honour. It is a symbol of Obsession.

♎ 16°. UNDER THE INFLUENCE OF THE PLANET
NEPTUNE.

> *A large hole out of which gases are rising.
> A number of birds seeking to cross are overcome
> by the fumes and are falling into the gap,
> over which only one has passed safely.*

Denotes one who will take many risks and often
expose himself to needless dangers. He should
be especially careful when near subtile substances,
gases, poisons, etc., and should always strive to
prevent others obtaining an undue influence over
him. Many travelling with him will fall by the
way, being ignorant of approaching dangers, but
he will *perceive*—let him regard his perception.
It is a symbol of Subtilty.

♎ 17°. UNDER THE INFLUENCE OF THE PLANET
NEPTUNE.

> *A beautifully formed foot rising from a haze
> of colour-waves.*

Denotes one artistic, thoughtful, and able, an
idealist of a highly sensuous nature whose labour
it is to blend material thought with spiritual

understanding, who perceives that beauty of form must melt into the sublimity of spirit. He will have powers as an inventor, for his inspirations are of a highly utilitarian nature, despite the Neptunian flights to which they ascend. It is a symbol of Sensibility.

♎ 18°.   UNDER THE INFLUENCE OF THE PLANET MARS.

A fireman rescuing a little child from a burning house.

Denotes one of a simple nature who is gifted with a strong spirit of self-sacrifice and endowed with inherent bravery. His way in life will be tangled at times, and he will need his energy to set it right again. He is a helper of himself and of others, and he does not count his own needs first. It is a symbol of Self-sacrifice.

♎ 19°.   UNDER THE INFLUENCE OF THE PLANET MARS.

A lion rising from the blood of a wounded soldier.

Denotes one of powerful and active mind and magical knowledge who knows the extent of his own force and ability, and, knowing it, he concentrates and suffers to give birth to an ideal of strength and nobleness combined—a strength and nobleness fitted to govern men and to demonstrate even to the weak that the concretion of abilities is the key to individual greatness. It is a symbol of Mastery.

♎ 20°.   UNDER THE INFLUENCE OF THE PLANET VENUS.

> *A young girl amidst the flowers in the sunlight wearing a garland of roses and weaving others.*

Denotes one to whom natural beauty offers the strongest appeal, whose happiness is in simple things, in art, literature, and science. Pleasure claims him only when pleasure is connected with the artistic. He can keep a secret better than he can keep his money and possessions, and he must be careful lest he be led into extravagances which can never appeal to his plain philosophy. It is a symbol of Gentleness.

♎ 21°.   UNDER THE INFLUENCE OF THE PLANET VENUS.

> *A flashily dressed woman singing, with a glass of wine raised in her right hand. On one side of her is the spirit of Mirth, on the other the spirit of Sorrow.*

Denotes one who is liable to be led astray by

externalities, who grasps at the shadow and misses the substance. Ornaments and the things which gratify the demanding senses only allure, but never satisfy, the continued demand for more. If in the government of himself he does not employ care and intelligence, he will find himself stung by a serpent, and the wound can never be healed. It is a symbol of Retribution.

≏ 22°. Under the influence of the planet VENUS.

> *A youth searching for a jewelled ring which he has on his finger.*

Denotes one who will waste time which, if he uses his mind and senses, he can save. He will be fairly favoured by fortune, will possess a dainty mind with an appreciation for all that is enlightening and charming, but there is a danger of negligence and lack of caution which will hurt him if he lets it. It is a symbol of Thoughtlessness.

≏ 23°. Under the influence of the planet MERCURY.

> *A pair of compasses lying on a map of the world.*

Denotes one whose business will demand movement and journeying. The native is a lover of travelling, for with him the rolling stone *does* gather moss and the still one but stagnation. He is a traveller and a searcher, seeking to know, not only this world, but that great beyond into which he also travels when sleep holds his mortal body. It is a symbol of Outreaching.

♎ 24°. UNDER THE INFLUENCE OF THE PLANET MERCURY.

A whirlwind scattering a mass of papers into the air.

Denotes one who will suffer from an over-confident nature that neglects those details which, insignificant as they may appear, are as necessary for the safeguarding of his interests as water is to earth. His mentality is good, and he is capable of useful mental work, but he may lose the results of his labours and suffer thereby in many ways. It is a symbol of Entrapping.

♎ 25°. UNDER THE INFLUENCE OF THE MOON.

A woman naked standing on a crescent moon, the stars glittering behind her in a sky of blue.

Denotes an attractive person who is in danger of being held in the chains of sense and at the will of others. His nature is impulsive and artistic, restless and pleasure-loving. His desires are

112

strong and may run riot with his reason. There is a leaning to the artificial, the theatre, and the dance, and a very sensuous love of earth life. It is a symbol of Vacillation.

♎ 26°.   UNDER THE INFLUENCE OF THE MOON.

A successful candidate for Parliament addressing the people after an election.

Denotes one who will gain from the masses. He is subtle, diplomatic, and capable of handling subjects from different view-points and in adhering to that interpretation which the majority believe to be correct. His philosophy teaches him to subordinate his ideas to the wills of those whose cause he champions. It is a symbol of Diplomacy.

♎ 27°.   UNDER THE INFLUENCE OF THE MOON.

The moon throwing its beams on a little bush hut amidst forest trees. A storm has just passed.

Denotes one who if saved from malefic planetary action is contented with little and is pleasant and kind to men and animals. His nature is devotional and sensitive, and is capable of obtaining knowledge from astral sources and atmospheric

113

conditions. He influences others for good, spreading content in the halls of inharmony. It is a symbol of Harmony.

≏ 28°. UNDER THE INFLUENCE OF THE SUN.

A mass of quartz through which veins of fine gold can be traced.

Denotes one to whom hard work appears to be the only thing worth while in this world, and who carries out his belief with himself as subject. He is conservative in his ideas and fights to uphold the landmarks of the fathers. It is a symbol of Exertion.

≏ 29°. UNDER THE INFLUENCE OF THE SUN.

An eclipse of the sun.

Denotes one who will have to be guarded in his dealings. With financial affairs great caution is necessary, for losses may occur of a serious nature, involving the native in much responsibility. He should never become surety for others, and should endeavour to realize himself and hold his earthly possession. Death will make inroads into his family circles and amongst near friends. It is a symbol of Fading.

LIBRA

♎ 30°. UNDER THE INFLUENCE OF THE PLANET
MERCURY.

A boy moping over his book in a schoolroom.

Denotes one who will have to wake up else he
will be elbowed out of everything by others more
vigorous.   He is possessed of good mental qualities,
is well-mannered and good-natured, but he allows
others to take advantage of him, and he will suffer
from deceit and unfairness.   It is a symbol of
Sluggishness.

SCORPIO

♏

♏ 1°. UNDER THE INFLUENCE OF THE PLANET MERCURY.

A man, enraged, tearing a book in pieces.

Denotes one of a passionate and determined nature. The personality is forceful and magnetic, but there is a lack of those fine feelings which render life something greater than a mere mass of disruption. It is difficult for the native to discipline and control himself, but his will is strong, and what is a fractious horse to a determined master ! It is a symbol of Irritation.

♏ 2°. UNDER THE INFLUENCE OF THE PLANET MERCURY.

Two men deeply engrossed in a game of chess.

Denotes one of excellent and discriminative brain who is capable of firm and continued concentration. The mind is intensely mercurial and penetrative, mastering difficult problems with comparative ease. It is a symbol of Comprehension.

116

♏ 3°.   UNDER THE INFLUENCE OF THE PLANET
MARS.

*Blacksmith striking anvil, the impact causing
a dazzling flash of bright light.*

Denotes one who strives to bring the light of
truth into a world of darkness.   It is not enough
for him gradually to secure acknowledgments—
individual minds won over, whilst useful, are not
what he most desires. He must arouse the
masses from their sleep, and the blow he strikes
on inert materialism will bring into action a light
more brilliant than the stars.   It is a symbol of
Penetration.

♏ 4°.   UNDER THE INFLUENCE OF THE PLANET
MARS.

Swordmaker tempering a sword.

Denotes one of skilful mind and aggressive nature
who desires to rise in life and lead, but who
recognizes the need of careful preparation and
planning before he ventures out.   When fortified,
he uses his inborn nature and tact, making sure
his weapons are keen and capable.   It is a symbol
of Preparedness.

♏ 5°. UNDER THE INFLUENCE OF THE PLANET JUPITER.

An ancient temple from which shoot forth forks of electricity.

Denotes one singularly gifted and of great power of observation who has ability to turn even the thoughts of old-world philosophies into forms of materialistic triumph. He is disposed to regard the thoughts of men and to ponder over, consider, and utilize what most people would cast aside as useless. Failures do not daunt his spirit, for he knows that success comes from repeated failures. He " attempts the end and does not stand to doubt." It is a symbol of Achievement.

♏ 6°. UNDER THE INFLUENCE OF THE PLANET JUPITER.

An eagle with a snake in its beak.

Denotes a forceful, determined character who will not be easily imposed on. A hater of deceit and mean actions, he silences the deception by crushing the deceiver. With himself he is continually at war, being swayed by two emotions, one uplifting, the other degrading. What he wishes to remain in mastery will remain. It is a symbol of Watchfulness.

118

SCORPIO

♏ **7°.** UNDER THE INFLUENCE OF THE PLANET JUPITER.

A winged horse flying over a fortress.

Denotes one whose destiny is to triumph over mere material force. One of great spirit, who will be enabled to demonstrate how much grander and how much more uplifting are the applied thoughts of man than the crude assertions and denials of materialism, no matter in what garb it may appear. His nature is free, his thoughts are free, and he desires to see all men aspire to true freedom and understanding. It is a symbol of Raising.

♏ **8°.** UNDER THE INFLUENCE OF THE PLANET SATURN.

A bundle of papers floating down a dark winding river under a starlit sky.

Denotes one whose object is to gain knowledge and who strives hard to attain his desires. In his dealings with others he holds the thought uppermost, and endeavours to turn the light of his acquirements on to material things. He has the ability to make his work on earth interesting and popular. He gains by deaths and certain work with others, but happiness will not be his so long as he holds the false light of materialism before

119

his eyes. His happiness is in the ideal, the true and only real. It is a symbol of Eagerness.

♏ 9°. UNDER THE INFLUENCE OF THE PLANET SATURN.

An ancient Hellenistic warship lying on the seashore.

Denotes one to whom ancient lore, poetry, and life strongly appeal, and whose soul goes back to those old days often in thought, often in sleep. But his nature is more positive than negative, and he can exhibit an aggressive or warlike front. He would do well to yield to his artistic nature and not allow the rustling of the wind to disturb his higher dreams. Let him let war rest like the old ship of the Greeks in the symbol, for the cruel days of war are passing. It is a symbol of Antiqueness.

♏ 10°. UNDER THE INFLUENCE OF THE PLANET URANUS.

A revolving star which throws off many colours and shades of colour.

Denotes one capable of receiving, translating, and presenting many shades of opinion, chiefly as regards philosophies or sciences with which he is identified. He is unorthodox in thought, but

120

reasonable, desiring not to condemn, but rather to enlighten, others. He may travel a great deal, but money does not cling to him, and he must avoid risks of all sorts. *His* wealth is in himself. It is a symbol of Discrimination.

♏ 11°. UNDER THE INFLUENCE OF THE PLANET URANUS.

Pretty little flowers growing on an old moss-covered wall in an old, green, country lane.

Denotes one poetical, intense, conservative, imaginative, idealistic, and artistic, one for whom simple beauty has a lasting and long appeal. His thoughts are above the narrow limits of form, creed, and custom, and his actions are marked by gentleness and feeling. The scientific vein in his nature is nurtured with the blood of Uranian science, and he is held but little to the wilder theories of some modern materialistic speculations. Whatever he handles must be dainty, sweet, and artistic. He loves children, flowers, the country, and all those things which lend grace and charm to earth life. It is a symbol of Serenity.

♏ 12°. UNDER THE INFLUENCE OF THE PLANET URANUS.

A galvanic battery resting on a rusty iron stand.

Denotes one of a strange and sensitive temperament—occult, thoughtful, and original. One who, like the battery in the symbol, will give shocks to many. He will have peculiarities and eccentricities, and will not be altogether easy to pull with, not that his temper is unkind, but that his vibrations are so fervent and his emotions so powerful. He is disposed to austerities and rigid rules of living which greatly influence others. It is a symbol of Immolation.

♏ 13°. UNDER THE INFLUENCE OF THE PLANET NEPTUNE.

Water bubbling over rocks and flowing into a large river.

Denotes one whose work is destined to live and influence men long after he has left the earth, one of an intensely psychic nature, sensitive, and mediumistic. He will have many earthly struggles and will find many sharp rocks in the way of his progress. He suffers more from his absolute lack of sympathy with earth matters as they are at present. His wanderings in the " summer lands," however, bring him infinite peace and joy in the midst of pain. It is a symbol of Reveries.

SCORPIO

♏ 14°. UNDER THE INFLUENCE OF THE PLANET NEPTUNE.

A lad pouring water into a sieve instead of a large jug, and watching two others fighting.

Denotes one whose mind is disposed to wander and to be distracted by the events of the moment. He needs to concentrate and to fight against the scattering of his thoughts. Ability he has, and can do well enough if he attends to one thing at a time. The tendency is to lose by carelessness what he earns by labour. It is a symbol of Distraction.

♏ 15°. UNDER THE INFLUENCE OF THE PLANET MARS.

A large ship ashore on an ironstone coast, waves dashing over her.

Denotes one disposed to travel and to delight in adventure and change. He has a vigorous personality, but is inclined to take from others more than he is willing to give. He will possibly attain a position, and his influence will sway many, but let him learn when to fall back into a more peaceful life, else will the great ship be cast on a dangerous coast by reason of strange influences, and disaster will be the end. It is a symbol of Conflict.

123

♏ 16°. UNDER THE INFLUENCE OF THE PLANET
MARS.

*An ancient warrior on his knees, with a cross-
sword stuck in the ground before him, praying.*

Denotes one who is mixed up in life's battles
and fights for every advantage. Gifted with
endurance and a penetrative mind, he wins his
way through obstacles only to meet more obstacles
later on. But he knows, for all this, that the
Power sustaining him is faithful, and he prays for
peace in the midst of war. It is a symbol of
Contrition.

♏ 17°. UNDER THE INFLUENCE OF THE PLANET
MARS.

*A dagger, with a jewelled hilt, stuck in a
document.*

Denotes peculiar birth conditions, but a gifted
person who, though threatened with danger,
overcomes and produces worthy works. His
powerful and energetic soul is blended with
idealism, poetry, and beauty. There is firmness
in all he does, and a power which gives it penetrative force and excellence. It is a symbol of
Romance.

124

SCORPIO

♏ 18°. UNDER THE INFLUENCE OF THE PLANET
VENUS.

*A ballet dancer who has just left the stage
talking to some men who are flattering her.*

Denotes one for whom pleasure hides danger.
His passions are high and not easy to control,
and his appetites tend to follow his desires.
There is a love of grace in art, movement, and
sound which impels him to excitement and
sensation. He attempts to influence and control,
but is liable to be deceived himself in the end.
Let him be warned. It is a symbol of Inflaming.

♏ 19°. UNDER THE INFLUENCE OF THE PLANET
VENUS.

*A woman, flashily dressed and adorned with
rings, bracelets, and numerous glittering jewels,
looking with longing eyes in a jeweller's window.*

Denotes one who is allured by the glitter of earth
as a moth is by the lamp glare. He finds it hard
to satisfy the yearning desire to possess and still
possess, like one of abnormal hunger who is
never satisfied. Let him take care lest this craze
grasp him body and soul, and grasping him makes
him the slave-victim of his passions. It is a
symbol of Retrograding.

♏ 20°. UNDER THE INFLUENCE OF THE PLANET MERCURY.

A handsome boy, climbing up a ladder, looking upwards to the heavens.

Denotes one especially favoured and of magnetic personality who raises himself by his own efforts and indomitable mind. He gains by right, scorning base and unworthy actions, and gains in spite of obstacles which are raised against him. He brings to others pleasure and help. It is a symbol of Determination.

♏ 21°. UNDER THE INFLUENCE OF THE PLANET MERCURY.

A double-headed giant, in his right hand a great club, in his left a tree—roots and foliage.

Denotes one who conceives the dualistic nature of man. He holds that the connexion of spirit and matter is the initial force from which all other forces are brought into being. He admits no intermediate force, pressing home his beliefs with all the certainty of proven facts and with all the vehemence his powerful nature is capable of. It is a symbol of Forcing.

126

SCORPIO

♏ 22°. UNDER THE INFLUENCE OF THE PLANET
MERCURY.

*A tax-gatherer demanding dues from a poor
poet.*

Denotes one who is forced by circumstances to
undertake duties which are not always of a
pleasant nature. His destiny is to adjust and to
demand, and the necessities of his life are opposed
to investigations of an ideal or psychic character.
It is a symbol of Gathering.

♏ 23°. UNDER THE INFLUENCE OF THE MOON.

A man blowing bubbles, a ledger at his feet.

Denotes one who is in danger of being misguided
and led into undertakings which can only result
in failure and regret. Should he attempt to
initiate any scheme himself, he will feel the
mortification of seeing his hopes shattered. He
should be content to take no risks. It is a symbol
of Uncertainties.

♏ 24°. UNDER THE INFLUENCE OF THE MOON.

*A wearied traveller on a hot, dusty road
obtaining a drink of water from a peasant girl.*

Denotes one who gives and receives, who loves
a roving life, and faces trials and hardships. But
no matter how hard the road may be, protection

127

comes before the journey's end. It is a symbol of Reciprocity.

♏ 25°.   UNDER THE INFLUENCE OF THE SUN.

A moneylender counting his gains in front of a safe crowded with valuables.

Denotes one who is lost in the maze of worldly gain and whose sole happiness is in his ever-increasing wealth. His nature is hard and his estimate of his fellow-creatures is judged by his own standard. His motto is : Treat every man as a rogue until you find him out to be honest, and when you find him out to be honest, think again before you trust him. It is a symbol of Hardness.

♏ 26°.   UNDER THE INFLUENCE OF THE SUN.

A pretty little bird standing on the back of a lion singing.

Denotes one of charming fancy, a singer of sweet songs, one of creative energy and personality. He is exposed to the craft of those in whom he has aroused feelings of envy, but he is under powerful protection and has little to fear. Let him sow seeds at the sun-rising part of life and be ready to gather the harvest in the setting. It is a symbol of Poesy.

128

♏ 27°. UNDER THE INFLUENCE OF THE SUN.

A king holding an illuminated sun's disc on a spearhead, speaking to his ministers.

Denotes one capable of lofty thoughts and high mental flights. There is a subtle, strong diplomacy about this native which cannot be easily gauged by others, but he *knows himself*, his own ambitious spirit, and his ever-growing faith—a faith which never wavers, no matter if he basks in favours or shields himself from frowns. It is a symbol of Distinction.

♏ 28°. UNDER THE INFLUENCE OF THE PLANET MERCURY.

A sailor steering a ship in a rough sea, looking anxiously ahead.

Denotes one of brave, adventurous, and scientific mind who will dare and do much to satisfy the demands of the curious. His life will be exposed to many dangers, most of which he will be prepared to meet, for he is the helmsman, and rough seas do not cause fear to him. It is a symbol of Adventure.

♏ 29.　UNDER THE INFLUENCE OF THE PLANET MERCURY.

A university professor lecturing to his students.

Denotes one of an entirely capable and trained mind who is enabled to throw some little light on the darker problems of life. He is fearless and cultivated, expressing theories and sticking to facts. His influence will sway many and his personality will win him confidence. It is a symbol of Performance.

♏ 30.　UNDER THE INFLUENCE OF THE PLANET VENUS.

A hand coming out from the heavens holding a pair of perfectly balanced scales, the star Venus glittering beneath.

Denotes one with a high ideal of true justice which to his mind is not possible without pure love. He is destined to send forth knowledge of a practical and philosophical kind which will help many along the stony way of life. He himself is a just and generous person, his principles guiding his acts in life. It is a symbol of Justice.

SAGITTARIUS

♐ 1. UNDER THE INFLUENCE OF THE PLANET VENUS.

A woman in the dress of a religious order struggling through a dark and storm-swept valley, a luminous anchor above her.

Denotes one of fine intellect who is gifted with persuasive eloquence. The native is poetic, reverential, and inspiring. He reaches a certain power and dignity after striving through worries and inharmonies. His will is firmly directed and cannot be broken, for above all he has faith in self and knows his own powers. It is a symbol of Triumph.

♐ 2. UNDER THE INFLUENCE OF THE PLANET VENUS.

A woman of angry countenance holding a dagger in her hand.

Denotes one strongly passionate and well favoured who finds it difficult to subdue and control the

131

forces by which he is swayed. Hence there is a tendency to do many regrettable things. He may be drawn into litigation and quarrels of various kinds, and may be tempted to aggressive action and threatening attitudes. Gradually, then, the finer side of his character will be hidden if not corrupted by the employment of the grosser. It is a symbol of Mutiny.

♐ 3. UNDER THE INFLUENCE OF THE PLANET JUPITER.

A man of scornful face with a big sword in one hand, carrying a child.

Denotes one over whose early life darkness hangs and who, if he escapes, will be involved in dangerous undertakings from which he will emerge triumphant or fall, perhaps not in vain. The mind is roused to intensity, and the native feels himself called to champion a great cause. He will follow with many followers. It is a symbol of Redressing.

♐ 4. UNDER THE INFLUENCE OF THE PLANET JUPITER.

Two arrows crossed and surrounded by zones of glistening violet light.

Denotes one who has a tendency to pull in opposite directions. The struggle between the

132

desires and right will be constant, and an act of hostility will be followed by deep remorse. It is a fight between the world of matter and the world of spirit. There may be peculiar changes in life, and that which is most unexpected is that which is most likely to happen. It is a symbol of Wavering.

♐ 5. UNDER THE INFLUENCE OF THE PLANET SATURN.

A dark bank of cloud passing in front of the sun, cutting its rays from the earth.

Denotes one of a melancholic, retiring, and occult nature who is drawn to a life of austerity, and whose search is for that hidden grail which holds the nectar of life and supreme knowledge. He is religious and sincere, but he should be careful lest his peculiar attitude or method of approaching the secret should hide it from his view, as the dark cloud-bank hides the rays of the sun. It is a symbol of Monasticism.

♐ 6. UNDER THE INFLUENCE OF THE PLANET SATURN.

A man in a black robe carrying a black rod on the top of which is a hand, the thumb held beneath the fingers of Jupiter and Saturn,

133

whilst the fingers of the Sun and Mercury are pointing upwards.

Denotes a powerful character of a religious and penetrating mind, by the virtue of which he rises to a position of enduring fame. Force, riches, and treachery oppose his power and influence, and may ultimately check, if not end, his career. But his actions will live and his spirit will rise above the power of reverses. It is a symbol of Valour.

♐ 7. UNDER THE INFLUENCE OF THE PLANET SATURN.

A large ship on a calm sea in a dark, starless night, a black bird of the raven order sitting on the mainmast top.

Denotes one whose position may be of some importance, but whose life will not be of any particular note, except in the manner of leaving it. He is not gifted with exceptional energy, nor with any particular ambitions, but he will meet with envy and hatred, from which he may suffer. He is by nature conservative, and will not easily yield to others. It is a symbol of Retaliation.

SAGITTARIUS

♐ 8°. UNDER THE INFLUENCE OF THE PLANET URANUS.

Draught horse pulling a load of chains up a hill, at the top of which is a great revolving wheel.

Denotes one who is limited, edged in, bound, and restricted, whose way is paved with difficulties which threaten and torment. He is exposed to dangers until after his seventh year, and if these are passed he is faced with a narrow way. He might remember the old Talmudic maxim, " Those whom God loves He oppresseth with suffering," and endeavour to grasp the purpose of his life. It is a symbol of Oppression.

♐ 9°. UNDER THE INFLUENCE OF THE PLANET URANUS.

A burning oil-well into which men are pouring quantities of water.

Denotes one gifted with a degree of mental richness, but who is somewhat diffusive and irregular. He has some remarkable qualities and good intellectual power, but is weak in application and method. Still he has wisdom, and can direct with magnetic forcefulness and purpose. It is a symbol of Retaining.

♐ 10°. UNDER THE INFLUENCE OF THE PLANET NEPTUNE.

A large metallic ball reflecting various colours.

Denotes one of a high order of intellect. He is naturally scientific, and gains recognition and esteem. He will be enabled to throw much light on obscure subjects and complex problems, and will win respect for his labours. He is highly inspirational, and embraces some school of occultism or uncommon thought. It is a symbol of Growth.

♐ 11°. UNDER THE INFLUENCE OF THE PLANET NEPTUNE.

A fisherman with a net over his shoulder sitting on a basket, a group of people advancing towards him.

Denotes a psychic of ability and reputation. He may hold some public position or come before the public in some way. The temper is somewhat jerky and the nature a little irritable, but he has good controlling power and a firm will. As a collector and publisher of knowledge this native has special genius. It is a symbol of Projection.

SAGITTARIUS

♐ 12°. Under the influence of the planet
Neptune.

*A coiled serpent, above which is a grinning
skull.*

Denotes one of a vicious temperament who is
liable to be obsessed and used by the dark forces.
A strong and beneficent power over him may
transmute his nature and aid him to overcome ill
fate, but evil is more likely to attend him and
make him her victim. It is a symbol of Over-
throwing.

♐ 13°. Under the influence of the planet
Mars.

*An archer, with blood-stained dress, shooting
at a stag.*

Denotes one of very strong vibrations and martial
nature who will have responsibilities and power
to fulfil them. He will meet with oppositions
and be exposed to considerable danger, especially
in the latter part of life. He is prophetic and
gifted in certain directions, but he must control
irritation in himself and soothe it in others. It
is a symbol of Provocation.

ZODIACAL SYMBOLOGY

♐ 14°. UNDER THE INFLUENCE OF THE PLANET MARS.

A human eye surrounded by a circle of flames.

Denotes one of penetrative power and clairvoyant gifts who will be well regarded by his associates and selected for positions of influence. He is naturally attracted to occult philosophy, uncommon learning, and that knowledge which concerns the coming into and going out of earth conditions. Peculiar magnetic and intensely active forces are associated with this degree. It is a symbol of Knowing.

♐ 15°. UNDER THE INFLUENCE OF THE PLANET VENUS.

A painter at his easel in a forest upland, observing not the heavy black clouds which betray an approaching storm.

Denotes one of a refined and sensitive spirit capable of becoming so absorbed in his studies that he detaches himself from the world and its peoples. The love of nature and the beautiful is very great and may sever his sympathy from the ordinary routine of earthly desires and ambitions. He may obtain excellence in his sphere and some degree of honour, but there is a fatality connected with this degree which will

138

claim him sooner or later. It is a symbol of Radiation.

♐ 16°. UNDER THE INFLUENCE OF THE PLANET VENUS.

> *A woman outside an old ruin under a starlit sky, a white angel on her right, a dark angel on her left. The stars—the lamps outside the palaces of the Holy Ones—are shining.*

Denotes one of intense mind capable of great acts. Very mediumistic, he is greatly influenced by his impressions and impulses. His path throughout his life is full of varied dangers, and he must be careful lest he miss the way. Let him often look up to the stars and pray for the guidance of the Good. It is a symbol of Restraint.

♐ 17°. UNDER THE INFLUENCE OF THE PLANET VENUS.

> *Cupid holding a broken arrow in his right hand and a miniature anchor in his left.*

Denotes one of an artistic and romantic temperament, fond of the poetic and beautiful and of that branch of science which lifts the soul of man beyond mere worldly limits up to the star-lands and the mountains of the moon. He may leave an enduring work of science, poetry, or romance.

139

Whatever he does he has faith in, and whatever he does hits the mark. It is a symbol of Imparting.

♐ 18°. UNDER THE INFLUENCE OF THE PLANET MERCURY.

A horse's hoof winged, crushing a butterfly.

Denotes one of great power of mind whose external thoughts threaten the glory of his soul. For his thoughts are powers which are ever striving to blend the spiritual and material in one great mould. He realizes to a great degree the potency of small things, and he is sensitive enough to feel acutely for suffering and to do all in his power to repel cruelty. It is a symbol of Subduing.

♐ 19°. UNDER THE INFLUENCE OF THE PLANET MERCURY.

A wand divided by a star.

Denotes one of philosophical force capable of manifesting from the silent hidden into the outer. Therefore his quality is explained in no ordinary terms. He has much personal force and magnetism which, if exerted for high ends, will become a harbinger for peace on this planet of experience and suffering. It is a symbol of the Awakening.

SAGITTARIUS

♐ 20°. UNDER THE INFLUENCE OF THE MOON.

A pleasure-boat on a picturesque river.

Denotes one who delights in the best the world can give and who strives to keep worry and trouble away at all costs. All that is beautiful in form, colour, and sound attracts him. He is a lover of ceremony and peaceful reveries, and his reputation in the arts that cultivate will be recognized, not, however, through any special power in himself, but just because it has to be. It is a symbol of Ease.

♐ 21°. UNDER THE INFLUENCE OF THE MOON.

A giant tidal wave.

Denotes one who from comparative obscurity raises himself to a position of influence. He is somewhat inconstant and uncertain, but he crushes opposition and all who challenge his way. He should be careful lest the force he uses be turned against himself, no matter how powerful he may be. It is a symbol of Onrushing.

♐ 22°. UNDER THE INFLUENCE OF THE MOON.

A dog on a wall baying the moon.

Denotes one restless in manner and uncertain in temperament who ever seeks for the unattainable and worries himself because he cannot get it.

In his cry, however, there is poetry ; poetry of a sad, hopeless strain as if foreboding some forlorn end to ambition, power, and aspiration. It is a symbol of Sighing.

♐ 23°.   UNDER THE INFLUENCE OF THE SUN.

A bee stinging a roaring lion.

Denotes one of sharp, stinging wit, of democratic feeling, and a fine order of intellect, who is bound to gain distinction of some kind. He will take a clear and extremely sensible view of things, and will be able to gauge and construct. The note of his sarcasm is directed against certain authority, and forces action when passivity seems firmly fixed. It is a symbol of Stimulation.

♐ 24°.   UNDER THE INFLUENCE OF THE SUN.

A bag of gold money falling into the ocean.

Denotes one who holds to the philosophy of fate and who will listen to no other. He makes mistakes and performs erratic actions. In money matters he should be extremely cautious, and he must not enter speculative fields, for heavy losses threaten him. He should hold what he can and trust in God and himself. It is a symbol of Mistakes.

142

SAGITTARIUS

♐ 25°. UNDER THE INFLUENCE OF THE PLANET
MERCURY.

*A ruined castle by a waterfall, near which is
a naked woman holding a bunch of grapes to
an old philosopher who, seated on a rock, is
studying a manuscript.*

Denotes one of romantic mind, loving and
leaning to the philosophy and thought of other
days, in which he is a master. The forces play
around him and attempts from the two worlds
will be made to draw him from his deeper
thoughts to the frivolity, folly, and transitory
joys of earth. Many times will he be shaken, but
his power is too great for sensual overcomings.
Instead he throws to the world the wine of life that
those who are able may drink. It is a symbol
of Spiritual Struggles.

♐ 26°. UNDER THE INFLUENCE OF THE PLANET
VENUS.

*Two girls on a see-saw gaily dressed, a man
in motley in the centre holding a cup of wine
in his hand.*

Denotes one who is attracted to the sport and
gaieties of life, and to whom physical pleasures
constitute the essence of existence. The native
may indulge in extravagances and will feel the

ups and downs of life. His philosophy favours the pursuit of happiness, and his mental gifts will be directed to the furtherance of his thoughts. It is a symbol of Pleasure.

♐ 27°.　UNDER THE INFLUENCE OF THE PLANET MERCURY.

> *Mercury holding up his caduceus in his right hand and with his left helping a fallen man to rise.*

Denotes one inspired and gifted, one prophetic, poetic, and artistic, whose mission it is to raise and uplift the race. He brings through the dark paths light and ecstasy, and those who hear the music will have their wounds healed. To see nature is with him to know nature, and the honey of wisdom flows from his mouth. It is a symbol of Eloquence.

♐ 28°.　UNDER THE INFLUENCE OF THE PLANET VENUS.

> *A simply dressed woman breaking a sword over her knee. In the heavens above masses of dark clouds are scudding before the rising sun.*

Denotes one possessing power, but utterly without bombast. To him war, quarrelling, and all
144

SAGITTARIUS

forms of inharmony, while abhorrent, are well inside the power of remedy. His nature inspires hope and security, and the dark threatenings of evil fly before this rising sun. It is a symbol of Benevolence.

♐ 29°. UNDER THE INFLUENCE OF THE PLANET VENUS.

A chariot, decorated with garlands of flowers, broken down on the roadway.

Denotes one to whom pomp, glitter, and show strongly appeal, combined with a love of travelling and pleasure. To such a one caution cannot be too strongly recommended. It is not a chariot gaily decorated which aids his power. Wealth combined with strength tells. It is a symbol of Vanity.

♐ 30°. UNDER THE INFLUENCE OF THE PLANET MARS.

A shield, with a gorgon's head embossed on it, attached to a column.

Denotes one of active mental power who is in-dispensable to his friends and a thorn to his enemies. He is capable of seeing events far in advance of their materialization and counts the

145

years of human progress in its pendulum-like motion. He has in him a strong spirit of fight and a feeling of naught else but victory. It is a symbol of Supremacy.

CAPRICORN

♑

♑ 1°. UNDER THE INFLUENCE OF THE PLANET MARS.

A man, armed, rising out of the earth.

Denotes one to whom power is given, especially connected with earthly science and knowledge. His passage through life will not be pleasured by calm and perfect peace. Rough seas and angry rocks will threaten him. As he grows older in years and experience he will know that combative science and theory but lead to unrest and fear. When this time comes he will truly arise out of the earth. It is a symbol of Disputing.

♑ 2°. UNDER THE INFLUENCE OF THE PLANET MARS.

A revolving disc of light, red centre surrounded by a black rim. The colours are pure and distinct.

Denotes a distinct personality of a martial, philosophic type, whose destiny it is to leave his

147

mark on the world's tablet. The influence favours elevation to a certain position of responsibility, but having reached this it is difficult for the native to retain it, and his restless spirit brings him into conflict with enemies of power who, if he be not cautious, will overthrow him. It is a symbol of Wrestling.

♑ 3°. UNDER THE INFLUENCE OF THE PLANET SATURN.

> *An old man seated on a throne in the clouds with his right foot on a sword. A large bright star is above his head and two pillars of light are on either side.*

Denotes one of genius whose gifts raise him far above the common things of earth, enabling him to comprehend sublimities. What he feels and knows he endeavours to clothe in a dress of vibrating colours to charm the children of earth and to raise them to dreams and contemplations of a glory beyond all material thought and understanding. It is a symbol of Immortality.

♑ 4°. UNDER THE INFLUENCE OF THE PLANET SATURN.

> *Persephone rising gracefully from the under to the upper world. The sun is shining, and*

the surrounding country is rich in fields of corn, fruits, birds, and flowers, whilst butterflies are sporting round her head.

Denotes one of great power of endurance who forces himself, ill or well, to brush away obstacles in the way of his desires. There is here a combination of mental, moral, and physical force, a trinity which carries the native through danger and conditions the most adverse. At birth the soul is rising from the shadows, and as life advances the temples of enchanting lights are reached, and constancy begets deathlessness. It is a symbol of Perseverance.

♑ 5°. UNDER THE INFLUENCE OF THE PLANET URANUS.

A winged urn from which water is pouring on to the parched earth. Where the water falls vegetation springs forth luxuriantly.

Denotes one of sympathetic and charitable nature, simple and charming, unorthodox, and free of religious and racial prejudice. The sordid fields of life have little hold on him, for his soul is expansive, eccentric even, and he hates pettiness. It is a symbol of Kindness.

ZODIACAL SYMBOLOGY

♑ 6°. UNDER THE INFLUENCE OF THE PLANET URANUS.

A traveller walking up a long forest rise, the path surrounded by dense gnarled trees. It is approaching evening, and the way is long and gloomy, but at the top can be seen a star within a wreath of fine clouds illuminating a beautiful blue sky.

Denotes one destined to lead in one of the great departments of life, but whose way will be threatened and whose heart will sometimes be faint. But even in the darkest times the lights of heaven will shine on him, stimulating him to action and accomplishment. His latter days may be days of faded flowers, but he will reach his star before his journey ends. It is a symbol of Manifestation.

♑ 7°. UNDER THE INFLUENCE OF THE PLANET URANUS.

A harp with broken strings, a scowling face above it.

Denotes one of ability whose career will be full of difficulties, mistakes, and threatenings. He is somewhat eccentric in manner, and will be led into action and argument from which he will gain no credit. He is susceptible in heart affairs,

150

is cultured, and loves the beautiful in its many forms.   If he would produce music, let him first string his harp.   It is a symbol of Jeopardy.

♑ 8°.   UNDER THE INFLUENCE OF THE PLANET NEPTUNE.

> *A woman looking on an empty cradle in an attitude of deep grief, the figure of a child near her, surrounded by a bright light, striving to pierce the gloom of her atmosphere.*

Denotes one whose life will be one of experience and who will suffer greatly through ignorance of certain knowledge which would free him if he knew it.   He should try and comprehend that the deeper the expressed grief, the harder it is for the truth to be known ; the blacker the darkness, the greater the danger into which he may walk.   It is a symbol of Admonition.

♑ 9°.   UNDER THE INFLUENCE OF THE PLANET NEPTUNE.

> *A man lying half asleep in a field, a veiled figure behind him with upraised hand.*

Denotes one born for great deeds whose work will be regarded many, many years after his exit from the narrow conditions of mortal life.   Gifted with inspirational powers and strongly impressed by powerful invisible forces, the native will be one of the many lanterns destined to throw light on this dark world. It is a symbol of Enlightening.

♑ 10°.   UNDER THE INFLUENCE OF THE PLANET MARS.

> *A glimmering light stealing into an old armoury, on the walls of which hang polished implements of war.*

Denotes one, active, ardent, and militant, whose enthusiasm will lead him into trouble or danger, and who is capable of heroic effort for an espoused cause.   The nature is by no means selfish, indeed the native would lay down his life for that which to him is right.   It is a symbol of Militarism.

♑ 11°.   UNDER THE INFLUENCE OF THE PLANET MARS.

> *An armed man riding on a lion, below him a scarabæus ; above, a mailed hand grasping an iron rod.*

Denotes one who by force and aggression gains position above his fellows, and holds it.   He will rise above the proud and force them to raise him higher, and his life and influence will be long.

152

CAPRICORN

There is much materialism in this native and much disregard for others. If he does not let the light enter his soul he may suffer from the force typified as an iron rod. It is a symbol of Undertakings.

♑ 12°. UNDER THE INFLUENCE OF THE PLANET MARS.

A man in full armour, visor up, holding his two hands on the hilt of his sword, the point of which pierces the ground.

Denotes courage and self-confidence. The native often meets danger or anxiety face to face, and is ever prepared to repel it when it comes. His sword is always ready, but he presses the point to earth, for he knows the power of the spirit, above all material force. It is a symbol of Striving.

♑ 13°. UNDER THE INFLUENCE OF THE PLANET VENUS.

A sublime spirit of female form holding by the hand a poorly attired child coming from the darkness into the mists and ascending from the mists into the light.

Denotes one who without regard to worldly condition will be aided and advanced to super-

153

earth state by a great protective agency, and the more the mind is raised to glorious contemplation the more closely will the heavenly cloak fall about his shoulders. It is a symbol of Guardianship.

♑ 14°.   UNDER THE INFLUENCE OF THE PLANET VENUS.

> *A woman in a drapery establishment, the table crowded with articles of dress, none of which please her.*

Denotes one not easily satisfied and who is not always conscious of the feelings of others. He is not deficient in taste, but he allows his mind to be so affected by varied desires and feelings that it is difficult for him to preserve firmness. He should ever strive to encourage the positive and to cultivate fixity of mind. It is a symbol of Dissatisfaction.

♑ 15°.   UNDER THE INFLUENCE OF THE PLANET MERCURY.

> *A hand extended, on which is resting a triangle, from which rays of light are issuing.*

Denotes one of fine comprehension and intellectuality, essentially fitted for very special world work. He is ever searching for the truth in art, science,

154

and life, and has a mind powerful enough to withstand criticism from the ignorantly learned. Reward comes to him. At the close of earth life he sees the light. It is a symbol of Transition.

♑ 16°. UNDER THE INFLUENCE OF THE PLANET MERCURY.

> *A number of books floating near a coast land rich in vegetation and floral charm, with beautiful grottos rising from the blue sea.*

Denotes one, artistic and nature-loving, who has a rapturous appreciation for the grandeur of creation and endeavours by some media—art, letters, or song—to express it. He has a strong affinity with nature, and her many moods will act and react on his sensitive soul. It is a symbol of Expression.

♑ 17°. UNDER THE INFLUENCE OF THE PLANET MERCURY.

> *A flood of deep blue light which, gradually becoming more and more refined, fades away altogether.*

Denotes one of sublime aspirations. To him the spiritual is ever more attractive than the material. The more life advances, the more refined his philosophy becomes until its rays fade from earth

155

with the soul so well expressing it.   It is a symbol of Supersensualism.

♑ 18°.   UNDER THE INFLUENCE OF THE MOON.

A silver-hued garment lying in the mud. Overhead are the dark clouds of an approaching storm.

Denotes one whose fate is greatly influenced by the acts of others, and whose life is blended with the hopes and ambitions of the many.   He will have trials and temptations, and can only defend himself and his honour by firmly refusing to be drawn into affairs of an unworthy nature.   It is a symbol of Changes.

♑ 19°.   UNDER THE INFLUENCE OF THE MOON.

A large crab with its claws embedded in a seal.

Denotes one of a vigorous and determined nature and great stubbornness of character who holds strongly to pronounced opinions and ideas.   If he is thrown into political life he becomes a statesman whose firmness will be appreciated by his friends and regretted by his enemies.   It is a symbol of Holding.

CAPRICORN

♑ 20°. UNDER THE INFLUENCE OF THE SUN.

A girl carrying a bowl of water into which are reflected the rays of the setting sun. All around is darkness.

Denotes one whose spirituality shines amidst the intensity of the darkness of materialism, a seer whose destiny it is to raise the fallen to a realization of the divine excellence of man and to warn off the dark and opposing enemies. It is a symbol of Evolution.

♑ 21°. UNDER THE INFLUENCE OF THE SUN.

The head of a goat with the solar disc between its horns.

Denotes an extremely sensitive and impressionable nature of romantic and strange fancies. If the sun is afflicted at birth or if the moon is changing from old to new, the native is liable to obsession or evil company, which threaten his honour, and he will have to seek help from more positive minds. But if the orbs be in good aspect and the moon be elevated, strong, advancing from new to full, advancement will be the native's destiny. It is a symbol of Perplexity.

♑ 22°. UNDER THE INFLUENCE OF THE SUN.

A hawk standing on a square black rock bathed in the rays of the rising sun.

Denotes one whose power is directed to the up-lifting and advancement of his race—a stayer of war and strife, of plague and riot. He looks directly ahead, far ahead into the years to come when the new sun will illuminate the glory of a new age of gold. It is a symbol of Renewing.

♑ 23°. UNDER THE INFLUENCE OF THE PLANET MERCURY.

A dog, holding a bird in his mouth, running across a field of daisies.

Denotes a far-seeing person with a fine apprecia-tion of poetry and the arts and a well-endowed mind capable of delving deeply into obscure subjects. Should Mercury be afflicted in the horoscope, especially by Saturn, the native will incline to exercise his powers in a wrong direction and to seek to restrain to his advantage the rights of others. It is a symbol of Sagacity.

♑ 24°. UNDER THE INFLUENCE OF THE PLANET MERCURY.

Three quivering arrows speeding towards a kneeling maiden, but before they reach her they crumble to atoms against a mighty hand which suddenly descends from the heavens.

Denotes one who will escape three great dangers by reason of a faith which draws to him the protection of the higher Powers. The most threatening is the third danger, but his faith is proof against this also. He will have moments of intense feeling and will not permit others to usurp his position nor rob him of the fruits of his toil. He is a peculiar child of destiny, and destiny does not design him for a low position in earth life. It is a symbol of Favour.

♑ 25°. UNDER THE INFLUENCE OF THE PLANET VENUS.

A man, gaudily attired, opening a document in the centre of which is a dagger.

Denotes one who will hold positions of responsibility and advantage. He has an inborn love of show and glitter, pomp and ceremony. He will be endowed with much mental ability and powers of persuasion, but is not free from secret enemies who seek to end his career by craft or violence. It is a symbol of Unrest.

♑ 26°. UNDER THE INFLUENCE OF THE PLANET
VENUS.

*A woman lifting from the ground an injured
child.*

Denotes one whose ruling impulse is for the
protection and comfort of mankind and who will
put this into practice ; in fact he will be called
upon to do so by the influence of that Power
who sent him to earth as a defender of the weak.
He will find himself in the midst of various
aiding and opposing forces, but so deep is his
sympathy with the oppressed that conquest is
sure unto him. It is a symbol of Tending.

♑ 27°. UNDER THE INFLUENCE OF THE PLANET
VENUS.

*A woman, neatly dressed, seated on an old-
fashioned chair, looking out of a cottage
window on to a pretty little garden. Her face
expresses pleasant contemplation.*

Denotes one of a particularly kind and gentle
temperament, extremely thoughtful and patient,
a lover of men, animals, and nature, of simple
tastes and careful judgment. The native has
psychic powers and prophetic foresight regarding
future events. It is a symbol of Meditating.

CAPRICORN

♑ 28°. UNDER THE INFLUENCE OF THE PLANET MARS.

An athlete throwing a large iron quoit and disregarding a wild, ill-conditioned dog who is barking at him.

Denotes one, vigorous in mind and body, who advances in his special sphere through his energy and by virtue of his destiny. He is sure to meet with enemies and opponents in life, and his way will be frequently threatened and challenged. But he is mysteriously protected, and so long as his intentions and actions are not stayed by the envy and criticisms of others all will be well with him. It is a symbol of Parrying.

♑ 29°. UNDER THE INFLUENCE OF THE PLANET MARS.

A dismantled fortress in ruins; near-by, an old man sitting on the ground, his back resting against a rock, with a sacred book beside him. His face expresses great sadness.

Denotes one of conservative and contemplative mind, aspiring, purposeful, and retentive, who mends the broken chains which link the past to the present, and who sees in the coming dawn a reflection of the remote past. He gains honour and esteem, but is not free from sadness. His

161

ideals will be injured by events, expected perhaps in all but intensity. It is a symbol of Comparison.

♑ 30°. UNDER THE INFLUENCE OF THE PLANET JUPITER.

A meteorite falling on a mountain-top.

Denotes one who is cautious and generally fortunate, and who nevertheless may be subjected to sudden attacks on his name and possessions. He should avoid law and legal tribunals, and should always fix agreements by writing, in order to prevent future disputes. He may gain a position of importance, but will not be able to hold it, or he may be elected to a position which can only be held for a limited term. The higher he aims the more he renders himself vulnerable to the shafts of those above him. It is a symbol of Strengthening.

AQUARIUS

≈ 1°. UNDER THE INFLUENCE OF THE PLANET JUPITER.

A human head in a mass of clouds, which are rose-tinted by the rising sun.

Denotes one of sensitive and poetic imagination who is capable of sublime flights of fancy. He is somewhat easily swayed by others, although himself capable of showing the way. He is a dreamer of dreams and a man of action, and many will have cause to honour his name. It is a symbol of Doing.

≈ 2°. UNDER THE INFLUENCE OF THE PLANET JUPITER.

A large mulberry-tree laden with fruit, around which are many birds.

Denotes one of romantic disposition and fine taste who will be favoured by fortune and who will attract many friends. There is benevolence and sympathy in this nature, and prophetic ability

163

also. He is generally successful in the attainment of his desires. It is a symbol of Contentment.

≈≈ 3°. UNDER THE INFLUENCE OF THE PLANET URANUS.

A white-haired man, holding a cross before him, walking over a mosaic pavement.

Denotes one of a truly religious mind whose career will be as full of incident as the many pieces which go to make a mosaic pavement are full of colour. Material life is not without its dangers —moral and physical—but the native is not born under the heel of fear. He sees beyond his times and bears his cross. It is a symbol of Faithfulness.

≈≈ 4°. UNDER THE INFLUENCE OF THE PLANET URANUS.

A beautiful fountain throwing upwards delicate sprays of yellow-tinted water, a jewelled crown showing in the mists.

Denotes one of refined mind who is destined to advance and gain power and influence over others. He will bring relief to many a thirsty soul, and many will bless him as he passes by the way. He is humanitarian, sincere, romantic, and harmonious. The life is not free from danger
164

until after the thirtieth year has passed. Thence his way is elevation and peace. It is a symbol of Defending.

≈ 5°. UNDER THE INFLUENCE OF THE PLANET NEPTUNE.

A nautilus shell being driven, on the sea, before the wind towards a rocky shore.

Denotes one who reaches fame fitting his rank. He will have elegant tastes and a love of luxury, but is liable to be imposed on or wrongly advised. He can quickly grasp impressions and set his thoughts into activity, but he should direct his will unto himself and watch the threatening rock-shore with his eyes well opened. It is a symbol of Inclining.

≈ 6°. UNDER THE INFLUENCE OF THE PLANET NEPTUNE.

A lady raising her white-gloved hand to receive a jewelled crown surrounded by a strange light which is floating towards her.

Denotes one on whom Fame smiles and who is fitted to receive her favour. For this native there is dignity and honour, which follows a degree of struggle, disappointment, and comparative obscurity. He is moved by many and varied

165

feelings and is blessed with a vivid and fine imagination. He is cultured, neat in style, and artistic. with considerable psychic ability and occult understanding. It is a symbol of Ascending.

≈ 7°. UNDER THE INFLUENCE OF THE PLANET NEPTUNE.

A naked foot bleeding ; above, a burning lamp.

Denotes one whose path in life will be filled with rocks and roughness, whose soul will be directed to the secret of the Holy Truth. He is liable to assaults, injuries, and the stings of jealous hate. Still he goes forward, forward like a conquering hero with light to lift the darkness and pain. He may falter, but he will not fall by the way. It is a symbol of Suffering.

≈ 8°. UNDER THE INFLUENCE OF THE PLANET MARS.

A soldier endeavouring to escape from a prison cell through a barred window.

Denotes one of a vital, vigorous, and martial disposition who endeavours to cut his way by mind or sword. Danger in early childhood may be overcome according to the power of the horoscope, but danger is never absent from him,

166

and he is liable to be constrained or oppressed with enemies of his own making or he may be a dangerous enemy to himself. To pass through a barred window self-conquest alone knows the way. It is a symbol of Limitation.

≈ 9°. UNDER THE INFLUENCE OF THE PLANET MARS.

A large, bright, military shield lying on a mountain, from which stream rays reflecting shafts of brilliant light.

Denotes one of powerful energy and firmness of purpose who in the second half of his life attains the reward of his labours and the gratification of his ambitions. He then attracts fame, drawing it unto himself as the loadstone draws steel. From his wisdom come rays which dazzle men by their brilliancy. It is a symbol of Reputation.

≈ 10°. UNDER THE INFLUENCE OF THE PLANET VENUS.

A woman, blind and in chains, in a magnificent and brilliantly lighted room.

Denotes one fated in the strongest sense of the term. If Venus is afflicted in the horoscope the native will be liable to suffer from over-indulgence of some kind or from some trouble

167

indicated by the Venusian position in the natal chart. He may do things he will regret and from which suffering may come. He should take hold of himself as a rider does a restless horse. Let him learn to open his eyes and to strike off his chains, and he will know the beauty which surrounds him. It is a symbol of Narrowness.

≈ 11°. UNDER THE INFLUENCE OF THE PLANET VENUS.

Flowers twined round a sceptre.

Denotes one of gifted mind and exceptional qualities, a singer of songs and a bearer of light, whose works gain for him respect and dignity, and whose name will be remembered long after his form has left this earth. Beautiful thoughts will cling to him as the ivy clings to the garden wall, and pleasant minds will come to him as the flowers which entwine the sceptre. It is a symbol of Taste.

≈ 12°. UNDER THE INFLUENCE OF THE PLANET VENUS.

A beautiful woman tending a dove with injured wing. On a table a manuscript, a bundle of letters, and an open book.

Denotes one of sympathy and feeling who thinks

168

deeply because he feels deeply, and whose ideas, entirely utilitarian, find the ready acceptance of the majority. He will have much to do with the launching of beneficial reforms, and will ever be striving to heal the wounds of others and point a way to go. It is a symbol of Reforming.

≈ 13°. UNDER THE INFLUENCE OF THE PLANET MERCURY.

A veiled figure, seated on a rock, pointing to a radiated human eye in mid-air.

Denotes one of occult understanding and a deep, feeling nature who will often be alone or apart from busy centres. Wherever he may be he never can *feel* really alone, for there is a power of seership bestowed on him which enables him to see the true, the beautiful, and the sublime in a form unknown to the masses of humanity. His is the eye that sees. It is a symbol of Discernment.

≈ 14°. UNDER THE INFLUENCE OF THE PLANET MERCURY.

Man writing, with a quill pen in each hand, in front of him a flickering oil-lamp. His face betrays anxiety.

Denotes one who strives to do more than he can accomplish, who has " too many irons in the fire,"

169

and, while thinking to accomplish much, does but little. He may be two-sided or have two philosophies obtruding themselves at the same time. The life is restless, anxious, and over it hangs a threatening hand. Peace comes from the cultivation of the higher and the rejection of the lower. It is a symbol of Difficulties.

≈ 15°. UNDER THE INFLUENCE OF THE MOON.

A woman seated on an anchor, a rudder in her hand and an opened book at her feet.

Denotes one who is guided through the many intricacies of life by a faith which cannot be shaken, being born of a philosophy or understanding which sinks deeply into a receptive nature. The mind is broad and wide in its sympathies, and the native feels and knows the reality of the way immortal, even though he may not be able to express it in mere words. It is a symbol of Guidance.

≈ 16°. UNDER THE INFLUENCE OF THE MOON.

A ship running before the wind with bare poles. The sea, black and angry, is illumined by a ray of moonlight which shines through a break in the heavy clouds.

Denotes one of a trusting spiritual nature who will

have trials in life threatening and bitter, and who will often be storm-driven and held in the grip of hard circumstances. Now and then there are breaks in the storms of life which bring relief, no matter how small. But he must go on ; his way is difficult and the night is dark, but in the morning light will come. It is a symbol of Experience.

≈ 17°.   UNDER THE INFLUENCE OF THE MOON.

A crab on an inverted triangle, above which are two hands tugging at a laurel wreath.

Denotes one of great perseverance who clings on to his ideas with a tenacity which forces respect. Things of earth worry him ; he will have to bear his cross, and he bears it without protest. He will not surrender, no matter how hard he may be pressed. He gains the victor's wreath in the teeth of opposition. It is a symbol of Strife.

≈ 18°.   UNDER THE INFLUENCE OF THE SUN.

A lion running along a dreary and barren field at the end of which is a V-shaped road. On the one side are hunters armed, on the other a rocky entrance leads to sunlit lawns.

Denotes a strong nature, capable of good or evil, who, after early struggles amidst uncongenial

171

surroundings, begins to perceive roads leading to some definite goal. According to the portents in the horoscope will the selected way be one of tears or smiles. There will be achievement of benefit or otherwise, and the earth end will be violent or peaceful as it is willed. It is a symbol of Doubting.

≈ 19°. UNDER THE INFLUENCE OF THE SUN.

Setting sun shining on a waterfall, giving it the appearance of golden water.

Denotes one who has a graceful method of expressing his thoughts and who will reach his place when life's midway has passed. He will accomplish much, and his words will ring so that many will stop to listen. His actions harmonize with his beliefs, and his soul is serene. It is a symbol of Proclaiming.

≈ 20°. UNDER THE INFLUENCE OF THE PLANET MERCURY.

A quaint old chest standing in an old hall, a large key on the floor before it. Around are pieces of armour and old instruments of music. On the top of the chest is a dog asleep.

Denotes one of a somewhat conservative nature, thoughtful, studious, and serious, by whom the
172

training of the mind is placed before all else and whose soul is set on works of cultivation. He may show special genius in some section of art or music, or he may be in a position to advance them. He is a seeker after truth and the key is near for him to use when the guardian has slumbered. It is a symbol of Skilfulness.

≈ 21°. UNDER THE INFLUENCE OF THE PLANET MERCURY.

> *A man with chains on his wrists appealing to a crowd of people.*

Denotes one whose life is set on the eradication of injustice and whose advocacy of what he considers right brings on him pain, ridicule, and misrepresentation. He is limited, chained, constrained, opposed, and oppressed, and will suffer hurt even from those for whom he gives up his comfort and ease. But the seal is set, and he will see the tree which many considered barren bearing fruit. It is a symbol of Heralding.

≈ 22°. UNDER THE INFLUENCE OF THE PLANET MERCURY.

> *A number of men saving volumes of books from the flames which are enveloping a library building.*

Denotes one of a literary and scholastic mind

to whom the pen is truly " mightier than the sword," and who inclines to the production of original works, whilst carefully preserving those that have gone before. In other ways he is a patron of literature and redeems much of value to the world. He may find himself in the midst of conflicting forces and be compelled to actions which may cause pain. It is a symbol of Conserving.

≈ 23°.   UNDER THE INFLUENCE OF THE PLANET VENUS.

A musician playing a curious instrument of the organ type. In the foreground a large St. Andrew's cross, one limb of a dark, cloudy substance, the other white.

Denotes one over whose early life a shadow hangs, of original mind, unorthodox and artistic. He is strangely moved by beauty and grace, blending loveliness of form with the seductive invisibility of sweet sounds. Living in the midst of high vibrations, the native is in danger of being drawn into the vortex of oppositions. Then the evil crosses the good and the devil wrestles with the man. It is a symbol of Crossing.

≈ 24°. UNDER THE INFLUENCE OF THE PLANET VENUS.

A woman neatly attired, with her hand on a tomb, looking sorrowfully on a flower-covered grave.

Denotes a refined person forced to meet sorrow face to face. According to the degree of experience to be learned, so will be the degree of sorrow to be endured. Passion is not apart from this degree, but passion leads to pain, whilst subjugation leads to mastery. It is a symbol of Tribute.

≈ 25°. UNDER THE INFLUENCE OF THE PLANET MARS.

A victor in a duel with a look of agony breaking his sword over his knee.

Denotes one born to conquer, but whose material conquests bring him pain and grief. As he advances in life and the sun of his soul throws brighter lights before him, he will realize how worthless aggression really is and how much grander is a word spoken in kindness than one spoken in anger, how much sweeter a kind face than one made hideous by the poison of hate. Then he will break his sword. It is a symbol of Reaction.

≈≈≈ 26°.   UNDER THE INFLUENCE OF THE PLANET
MARS.

*Three fires blazing above three triangular hills,
a cross sword floating in air above.*

Denotes one of mystic and reformative leanings
who may be impressed by invisible forces for
certain work on earth, but who may not be
conscious of the part he is called upon to play.
He has intelligence, force, and bravery, with a
strong will, and what he is willed to do he will do.
He should never permit himself to be hypnotized
nor entranced, nor yield his will to the power of
another, in the body or out of it.   It is a symbol
of Service.

≈≈≈ 27°.   UNDER THE INFLUENCE OF THE PLANET
MARS.

*A man of strong build locking securities in a
great iron safe in the turret-room of an old
castle.*

Denotes one, forceful, strong, and aggressive, who
will be the guardian of many responsibilities
and who unites strength of purpose with executive
ability.   He defends and attacks : he is a master
and a servant.   Errors are always dangerous,
and only from errors will regret come.   It is a
symbol of Stewardship.
176

≈≈ **28°.** Under the influence of the planet
Jupiter.

*A spire on top of a pyramid, at the base of
which is a horse with a manuscript in his mouth.*

Denotes one born for great deeds, aspiring and
energetic. His work will travel far and will be
of a strong and reformative character, which will
meet with the usual opposition afforded to such
works amongst a certain caste. He must never
stay. Ever with the symbol before his eyes must
he continue his way, for victory is sure. It is a
symbol of Reformation.

≈≈ **29°.** Under the influence of the planet
Jupiter.

*Forked lightning surrounded by stars amidst
storm-clouds.*

Denotes one whose rise in life will be sudden
and who will maintain his position with difficulty.
He will enjoy the smiles of favouring fortune and
suffer the frowns of envy, and is destined to
wrestle with opposition and inharmonious conditions. Let him study his horoscope and steer
clear of the breakers. It is a symbol of Debate.

≈ 30°.   UNDER THE INFLUENCE OF THE PLANET SATURN.

Wavy rays of light, in shape like a huge wheel, reflecting on a blue evening sky.

Denotes one of sober judgment and a natural leaning towards the occult arts. He has respect for such learning, in which he himself is gifted. His logical nature refuses to be led by orthodox thought or to yield to the shallow opinions of hypnotized crowds. Generally the life is fortunate. The native is slow to move, but has abundant sympathy, which his mind regulates or restrains. As he advances in earth life, his psychic eye will be opened and he will know and understand those things which he before accepted with reserve, but without scruple. It is in the latter part of his life that the gates of knowledge are opened to his soul. It is a symbol of Controlling.

PISCES

♓ 1°. UNDER THE INFLUENCE OF THE PLANET SATURN.

A satyr sitting on a rock by a river which is running into the sea, holding a fish.

Denotes one of a peculiar disposition who is in danger of yielding to the suggestions of evil influence and being guilty of unjust actions. He may suffer sorrow from or through relatives and from secret affairs, and he may not be able to do just what he pleases. He has strong promptings towards the occult and hidden arts. It is a symbol of Misgiving.

♓ 2°. UNDER THE INFLUENCE OF THE PLANET SATURN.

An old man sitting beneath a leafless tree with bread in his hand and a bag of money by his side.

Denotes one who will be no stranger to suffering. Directly or indirectly he benefits through people

179

older than himself. No matter how important his position in life, he is limited. He feels for those whose portion of earth life is but pain and he relieves when the pained plead. It is a symbol of Clemency.

♓ 3°. UNDER THE INFLUENCE OF THE PLANET NEPTUNE.

The deck of a trawler on which are quantities of fish. It is night, a small cottage is on fire on the land, and this, with the shore lights, is reflected in the water.

Denotes a strong character, a leader in his sphere of life. Dangers from the elements threaten the child life. He has the ability to grasp and utilize the ideas and suggestions of others, and his power of observation enables him to advance his interests and obtain reward. He will be successful in secret negotiations, and secret matters largely affect the life. It is a degree of Secretiveness.

♓ 4°. UNDER THE INFLUENCE OF THE PLANET NEPTUNE.

A lighthouse built on rocks in the midst of an angry sea. Over the sky is a rainbow.

Denotes one who will be placed in the midst of unsettled chaotic conditions and who, as com-
180

plication after complication arises, allows fear to hold him. Yet he is secure against storms and firm against disaster, although not from assault. He has mediumistic power to enable him to know his inward strength, but he fears to use it. If he would but turn his eyes upwards he would see beauty above fear and ever have hope before him. It is a symbol of Mistrust.

♓ 5°. UNDER THE INFLUENCE OF THE PLANET MARS.

The interior of a tent of a Roman military commander, in which is a table set with abundance of food and drink in rich vessels of gold and silver.

Denotes one of good organizing and directing ability who works with a purpose in his mind and an ideal at heart. He has a love of luxury and good living, and as life advances he will be in a position to gratify his desires. He is a good, generous friend, and gains esteem. He does not allow personal comfort to affect the work he is called upon to do nor to diminish his personal courage. It is a symbol of Accomplishment.

♓ 6°.   UNDER THE INFLUENCE OF THE PLANET MARS.

> *Pirates tying a captive to a tree by the seashore. An old sailor hidden behind the rocks and foliage watching and waiting, knife in hand, to set him free.*

Denotes an adventurous nature which will attempt rash things and undertake dangerous missions. The native is in danger of restraint and attack from powerful foes seeking to put him out of action, but is fortunate in obtaining relief when he least expects it.   From the twenty-seventh to the twenty-eighth, the thirty-sixth to the thirty-seventh, are critical years. It is a symbol of Attempting.

♓ 7°.   UNDER THE INFLUENCE OF THE PLANET MARS.

> *Two wrestlers struggling for mastery.   One is dark and evil-looking, whilst the other is as an angel in manly beauty.*

Denotes the dark and treacherous forces and the materialism of man combating with all that is glorious, all that is ideal and divine.   To whichever the thoughts of the native incline comes victory, and many times in life he will be forced to join himself to the one or the other.   May

182

wisdom direct his choice. It is a symbol of Contesting.

♓ 8°. UNDER THE INFLUENCE OF THE PLANET VENUS.

A slave-merchant selling a beautiful woman in an Eastern market-place.

Denotes one who is destined to have power over others and who may be forced by circumstances to obey the wills of stronger forces. Necessity may compel him to barter his dearest possession for external advantage, but those to whom he barters it prize it. His is a peculiar life of importance, but not one of absolute free will. It is a symbol of Responsibilities.

♓ 9°. UNDER THE INFLUENCE OF THE PLANET VENUS.

Venus and Cupid, metamorphosed as two fishes, swimming from a giant who stands on a rock.

Denotes one of a sensitive disposition and pure mind who understands intuitively the true meaning of love as symbolized in the planet Venus, sublime and in her dignity. His enemy is lust, which threatens to cling to him and by craft to hold the throne of his soul in the guise of love. But

183

the native will know vice as a destroying angel only, and his knowledge will protect him and set him free. It is a symbol of Transmutation.

♓ 10°. UNDER THE INFLUENCE OF THE PLANET MERCURY.

A man sweeping together quicksilver which has fallen from a dish and has scattered in all directions.

Denotes one of an active, volatile mind, alert and restless, possessing knowledge and the power to acquire knowledge. There is, however, danger of his ideas leaving him and being scattered in parts where they are not appreciated. When he fully recognizes the gift with which he has been blessed he will by concentration draw it unto himself and bestow it on those who will hold it to advantage. It is a symbol of Teaching.

♓ 11°. UNDER THE INFLUENCE OF THE PLANET MERCURY.

A dog running amongst some children playing on the seashore.

Denotes one of sagacious mind, very faithful when trust is given, and active in the carrying out of any mission he is entrusted with. There is determination in the character, and the external

184

appearance betrays but little the feelings and emotions. He acts with caution, craft, and confidence, and is generally friendly. It is a symbol of Alertness.

♓ 12°. UNDER THE INFLUENCE OF THE PLANET MERCURY.

An author with his head in his hands, a rejected manuscript and a lady's photograph on a table before him.

Denotes one of literary or artistic ability who attains a degree of reputation and esteem, but who is tempted by the smiles of alluring love. He will reach a stage when he will be compelled to decide between two mistresses, one as insistent as the other. It is a symbol of Intricacy.

♓ 13°. UNDER THE INFLUENCE OF THE MOON.

A man crossing a bog on an old tree which has long ago fallen.

Denotes one who meets with public favour and support whose temper will be severely tried and tested. Although possessed of radical feelings, he will find himself compelled by circumstances to obtain conservative support even though that support be grudgingly given. Still it will serve. It is a symbol of Preserving.

185

ZODIACAL SYMBOLOGY

♓ 14°. UNDER THE INFLUENCE OF THE MOON.

A number of stevedores loading a ship at a port.

Denotes one who sees prayer in labour and nobility in work. No matter what may be his station in life, his beliefs will be strongly democratic and just. There may be a good deal of moving about during life or a long voyage may take the native into lands remote from his place of birth. He is sincere, and can be relied on. It is a symbol of Activity.

♓ 15°. UNDER THE INFLUENCE OF THE SUN.

A man standing on a high look-out, nervously scanning the horizon at high noon, a comrade falling at his side stricken by the sun.

Denotes one gifted with keen powers of observation who gains a position of usefulness and responsibility. His life will at times be unsettled, and his advancement will be in the hands of others. He may be threatened with disfavour, illness, or accident. He should banish irritability or nervousness, for such cause trouble. Still he is always sincere. It is a symbol of Trustworthiness.

PISCES

♓ 16°.   UNDER THE INFLUENCE OF THE SUN.

A hawk with outspread wings standing on a trumpet.

Denotes one of fearless disposition and venture-some nature who makes a big throw for fortune and who reaches a point of notoriety or fame in the face of obstacles, opposition, and envy. Favours come from authority, but dangers from falls, fire, and sword are threatened. It is a symbol of Renown.

♓ 17°.   UNDER THE INFLUENCE OF THE SUN.

A gaudily dressed officer holding aloft a spear of gold.

Denotes one of magnetic force, patience, and determination who wins his way by sacrifice of self for the sake of his ambition and who will never rest until he has achieved his purpose. He is identified with a great cause or a great pro-duction, spreading knowledge or giving pleasure. It is a symbol of Announcement.

♓ 18°.   UNDER THE INFLUENCE OF THE PLANET MERCURY.

A spider seizing a fly caught in the web.

Denotes one who may be deceived in many

important concerns of life and who should be especially careful in giving confidences and in betraying his affairs to others. He should avoid law and all forms of litigation and contention, and should not accept too lightly the opinion of others concerning his business. It is a symbol of Temptation.

♓ 19°. UNDER THE INFLUENCE OF THE PLANET MERCURY.

A sick man lying at the base of a large stone cross, a greyhound running in the distance.

Denotes one of great faith which, being added to true knowledge, makes man invincible. The mind inclines to religion and charity, and is well endowed. Generally he is quick to grasp matters and to profit by his wisdom. He suffers some discomfort in life and many disappointments. Ill-health may also trouble him. Still, he has faith, and faith can truly move mountains. It is a symbol of Believing.

♓ 20°. UNDER THE INFLUENCE OF THE PLANET VENUS.

An itinerant musician playing the mandolin and singing love-songs to a number of country maidens who are seated on rocks and fallen trees around him.

Denotes one who is musical, artistic, and pleasure-loving who is gifted with a wealth of imagination and an engaging manner. He gives pleasure to many, and will meet with much applause. His nature is light and airy and somewhat wanting in stability. He delights to wander about, or his calling may involve much travelling. It is a symbol of Entertaining.

♓ 21°. UNDER THE INFLUENCE OF THE PLANET VENUS.

A staff adorned with coloured ribbons, standing in a field of violets, butterflies circling around it.

Denotes one of a fresh and beautiful mind, a lover of nature in sunshine and shower. His ideal is a life of freedom in flowered fields and woods. He inclines to people of high thoughts, children, animals, and the great things of life. He will be exposed to some dangers and will sometimes find the way blocked—the way he has to go. Still, a magical protection is over him and a defending power invisible is always near. It is a symbol of Shielding.

ZODIACAL SYMBOLOGY

♓ 22°. UNDER THE INFLUENCE OF THE PLANET VENUS.

A snake hidden in a bush of wild flowers near a bubbling stream.

Denotes one of wandering and inconstant nature who has cause to fear the tyranny of his senses. He will in turn be the deceived and the deceiver, and when he attempts to deceive others he deceives himself most. His nature is of the romantic tinge. He loves music and song, the theatre and the ballet, and appreciates the beautiful. If he dare, he may redeem himself. It is a symbol of Ensnaring.

♓ 23°. UNDER THE INFLUENCE OF THE PLANET MARS.

A heap of broken arms and military trappings lying in a muddy pool.

Denotes one who will know the poverty of aggression and who will suffer from the effects of his actions and intentions. He will understand that what is gained by force may become a curse instead of a blessing, and why the so-called glories of ancient Rome became so many daggers at her throat when the results of her deeds brought her to earth. Let the native prove his power in a greater way than by contention. Let him clear

190

his mind and control himself if he can. It is a symbol of Militancy.

♓ 24°. UNDER THE INFLUENCE OF THE PLANET MARS.

A giant ape dragging a woman into the forests.

Denotes one who is in danger of becoming a slave to his desires and to sacrifice his higher self to the exhausting excesses which eat into body and soul. There is a wasting of energy and power in the pursuit of so-called pleasure which deprives the native of that perfect idealistic happiness which is gained by sweet restraint and a knowledge of perfect love. It is a symbol of Falling.

♓ 25°. UNDER THE INFLUENCE OF THE PLANET JUPITER.

An unfurled flag on a shaft of forked lightning.

Denotes one of nervous, quick, and restless temperament, impulsive, active, and full of energy and purpose. His nature is brave and defiant, and his life will not be free of adventure of some kind. He will always be beyond want and his position will be secure. Events in his life happen abruptly and are not always expected. It is a symbol of Suddenness.

♓ 26°. Under the influence of the planet
Jupiter.

> *A dowser, with a wand of hazel in his hands,*
> *finding water on barren lands.*

Denotes one who will be blessed with natural gifts
of a very high order. He will be very fortunate
in his undertakings, benevolent, and beneficial
to the people. He is a searcher and a seeker, is
rather conservative, and does not easily accept reforms and changes. It is a symbol of Discovery.

♓ 27°. Under the influence of the planet
Jupiter.

> *A horse running, with flames issuing from his*
> *nostrils.*

Denotes one who has special work to do and whose
name will be associated with important projects.
His nature is passionate, quickly receiving and
recording spiritual impressions. The disposition
is kindly. He is well disposed, and his sense of
justice is strong. It is a symbol of Directing.

♓ 28°. Under the influence of the planet
Saturn.

> *A black cat sitting on an old parchment-covered*
> *book.*

Denotes one who, if he live beyond infancy, will

rise to a position of some responsibility. Blessed with superior gifts, this native will be esteemed for his wisdom and understanding. He leans towards old things and will reflect the tendencies of his ancestors. He receives favours from old people and has fortunate dealings with others. It is a symbol of Firmness.

⋎ 29°. UNDER THE INFLUENCE OF THE PLANET SATURN.

A bat flying at night in an old graveyard.

Denotes one who endures sorrow. He should strive to force himself away from lowering tendencies by mingling with cheerful and fine-minded people and by studying the true nature of thoughts, feelings, emotions, and strange happenings in one of the occult schools to which he most inclines. He should always guard against jealous feelings in himself and in others. It is a symbol of Sadness.

⋎ 30°. UNDER THE INFLUENCE OF THE PLANET URANUS.

A man trudging along a rough road, dragging a mass of heavy chains. A strong horse in a cart standing idly near.

Denotes one who undertakes needless labour

193

and who binds himself in chains of his own making. He has peculiar ideas, thoughts, fancies, and eccentricities, and the regulation and control of these and the cultivation of his powers of observation will lead him to the understanding of great things and open a gate which is at the beginning of the perfect way so opposed to the rough road of selfish materialism on which the majority of the world's people have been content to travel till the closing of their earth lives. It is a symbol of Misconception.